HONEST MONEY

Other books by Gary North

Marx's Religion of Revolution, 1968
An Introduction to Christian Economics, 1973
Unconditional Surrender, 1981
Successful Investing in an Age of Envy, 1981
The Dominion Covenant: Genesis, 1982
Government By Emergency, 1983
The Last Train Out, 1983
Backward, Christian Soldiers?, 1984
75 Bible Questions Your Instructors
    Pray You Won't Ask, 1984
Coined Freedom: Gold in the Age of
    the Bureaucrats, 1984
Moses and Pharaoh, 1985
Negatrends, 1985
The Sinai Strategy, 1986
Unholy Spirits: Occultism and
    New Age Humanism, 1986
Conspiracy: A Biblical View, 1986
Inherit the Earth, 1986
Fighting Chance, 1986 [with Arthur Robinson]

Books Edited by Gary North

Foundations of Christian Scholarship, 1976
Tactics of Christian Resistance, 1983
The Theology of Christian Resistance, 1983

HONEST MONEY

The Biblical Blueprint
for Money and Banking

Gary North

DOMINION PRESS • FT. WORTH, TEXAS
THOMAS NELSON, INC. • NASHVILLE, TENNESSEE

Co-published by Dominion Press, Ft. Worth, Texas, and Thomas Nelson, Inc., Nashville, Tennessee.

Printed in the United States of America

Unless otherwise noted, all Scripture quotations are from the New King James Version of the Bible, copyrighted 1984 by Thomas Nelson, Inc., Nashville, Tennessee.

Library of Congress Catalog Card Number 86-050796

ISBN 0-930462-15-7

This book is dedicated to
John Mauldin
who has assured me, as my director of marketing,
that this book will make me a pile of money . . . honest!

TABLE OF CONTENTS

Part I
BLUEPRINTS

We began by stating that the issue with respect to gold is an issue more centrally with respect to God. Is there an ultimate and absolute order, and does God's sovereign law establish an inescapable order with respect to every sphere, so that transgression of that law brings social penalties and decay? Or is humanism true, and the only value is man and his desires, his pleasure in consumption, display, and expression? The monetary crisis reflects a cultural crisis.

Those opposing welfare economics must of necessity have a sound monetary policy. But a sound monetary policy rests in the framework of absolute law, in the basic premise of the sovereign and absolute God whose law-order governs all reality. Without this faith, the conservative's economics lacks the consistency of the statist's. The monetary policies of socialism reflect, after all, a consistent faith in the ultimacy and sovereignty of man and man's ability to create his own law, money, and world at will. Here as elsewhere the question is simply this: who is God? If the Lord be God, then follow Him. But if Baal be god, then Baal must be followed. Not without significance, the U.S. coinage, from the days of the Civil War, bore the imprint, "In God We Trust."

R. J. Rushdoony*

*Rushdoony, *Politics of Guilt and Pity* (Fairfax, VA: Thoburn Press [1970] 1978), pp. 241-42.

INTRODUCTION

This is a book on money, a subject that has defied analysis by professional economists for as long as there have been professional economists. At the same time, it is a topic for which the most ill-informed people think they have the answers. Very often the most ill-informed people are professional economists.

I will give you an example. In the fall of 1985, I suggested to a research assistant to a U.S. Congressman that he conduct a quick study of the Mexican peso. I thought that the sharp increase in cash American money in circulation, 1982-85, might be explained by Mexican nationals substituting dollars for pesos in Mexico. At the time that he began his investigation, the peso was selling for about 250 per dollar. I suggested that he ask a staff economist at the Federal Reserve System, our nation's central bank, if he thought that Mexicans were hoarding cash dollars. I suspected that Mexican citizens were using the U.S. dollar as a substitute for the collapsing peso.

He phoned back a few days later. Two staff economists, one of whom was a specialist in the Mexican economy, had told him that it was quite unlikely that Mexicans were hoarding dollars, because Mexicans could take cash dollars to their local bank, exchange their dollars for pesos, and the bank would pay them interest in pesos.

Within one week, the peso fell to 500 to the dollar. Thus, anyone who had followed the advice of the expert economists had lost half of his capital. On the other hand, those who had bought cash dollars with their pesos and never went near a bank had doubled their money (pesos). In short, a lot of illiterate Mexican peasants know more about practical economics in an inflationary economy than Federal Reserve economists know. Somehow, this discovery did not surprise me.

A few months later, a report on the apparent disappearance of American cash appeared in the newspapers. It said that Federal Reserve economists now think that people in foreign countries are using American bills instead of their depreciating national currencies. So much for the consistent views of economists. They just don't agree on much of anything, except the need to keep economists on the payroll.

The Crisis We Face

There is a debt crisis in the making. It is international. Every industrial nation on earth faces a crisis that could dwarf the crisis of the 1930's. The banks of the world have done the bidding of the politicians, and they have loaned hundreds of billions of dollars and other currencies to the "less developed countries (LDC's)." The politicians wanted them to do this because the voters were tired of sending government foreign aid to these backward socialist dictatorships and tribal despotisms. Beginning in the 1970's, the bankers sent the depositors' money by the hundreds of billions of dollars.

The result in either case is the same: the money is gone. The despots bought what they wanted, and squirreled away hundreds of millions or even billions in Swiss banks. (In early 1986, the Swiss government froze the bank accounts of deposed Philippine President Marcos when it was rumored that he was about to pull "his" money out of Swiss banks.) The governments built cities (the classic example is Brasilia) and power plants and steel mills — none of which produces a profit. The money was spent, the pyramids were built, and now the West's banks are sitting on top of a mountain of IOU's that are never going to be paid off, at least not with money that is worth anything.

This means that you and I are sitting on top of those IOU's, for it was our economic futures that the idiot bankers gave away. But it's partially our fault; we trusted them, year by year.

There are no solutions. The loans are sour. There will be a default. The practical forecasting questions we need to get answered are these: How soon will the default come? What kind of default will it be?

This book asks a different question: What violations of the principles of the Bible did the West commit that led us into this mess? It also asks this question: What should we build on the ruins of the present system after the collapse?

Biblical Alternatives

There are Biblical alternatives. If we had adopted them 500 years ago, or 100 years ago, or even 50 years ago, we would not be facing the monetary crisis that we now face. But we didn't adopt them, so we are facing it.

Professional economists do not take the Bible's answers seriously. They will not take this book seriously. But we have listened to professional economists for 200 years, and what do we have to show for it? Where have they set forth a simple, principled, clear program for long-term economic stability? Where have they come to any agreement on what ought to be done? Nowhere. Where there are five economists, there will be at least six opinions.

Professional theologians who believe in the Bible as the infallible Word of God also have not taken the Bible's answers seriously. They are not used to thinking of the Bible as a book that offers social, political, and economic blueprints. They have not concerned themselves with broad social questions for over a century.

Why, then, do I think I know the things the Bible says we must do, when the atheistic economists and let's-not-get-involved-in-social-issues theologians are agreed that the Bible doesn't offer us any specific blueprints? Because I take the Old Testament seriously. The economists and the let's-just-preach-Jesus theologians don't.

When the crises hit—and they *are* going to hit—Christians need to be in positions of leadership, ready with accurate answers about how and why the crises hit, and what the Bible says needs to be done to recover from them, and to keep these crises from hitting us again. This means that Christians need to understand the Bible's blueprints for every area of life. One of these areas is monetary policy.

The principles of honest money are not difficult to learn. Implementing them, on the other hand, will involve considerable social cost, but nothing compared to what the West will go through if we Christians don't do the work, and the civil government doesn't begin to enforce God's law. If we fail to reconstruct the present banking system because everyone refuses to pay whatever social costs are necessary to do it, we will eventually pay far higher costs anyway. Christians should be prepared to follow Jesus' warning about counting the costs:

> For which of you, intending to build a tower, does not sit down first and count the cost, whether he has enough to finish it—lest, after he has laid the foundation, and is not able to finish it, all who see him begin to mock him, saying, "This man began to build and was not able to finish" (Luke 14:28-29).

1

THE VALUE OF MONEY

So when the money failed in the land of Egypt and in the land of Canaan, all the Egyptians came to Joseph and said, "Give us bread, for why should we die in your presence? For the money has failed" (Genesis 47:15).

Daniel Defoe wrote a novel in 1719 about a man whose ship sank, and who wound up on a deserted island for 28 years. It was called *Robinson Crusoe*. Economists love to use Robinson Crusoe as their example when they begin an introductory textbook on economics. Why? Because he was alone initially. We can then talk about scarcity and its economic effects in a world without a money economy. Why didn't Crusoe's economy have money? Because it was a world without exchange (trade) and the division of labor.

Crusoe faced a hostile world. How was he going to overcome scarcity? He needed food, clothing, and shelter. Fortunately for him, he was able to get a lot of his tools from the ship; if he hadn't, he wouldn't have survived even 28 days.

The reason why economists use Robinson as an example is that they don't have to begin with the difficult problems of the division of labor and voluntary trade. Only when the economist has explained basic production, saving, and the allocation of time and capital does he introduce Friday, the native partner. That was Defoe's strategy, too.

The textbook Crusoe initially has to decide what his highest priorities are. What is his order of preferences? Is it fresh water, food, shelter, or clothing? What need does he attempt to satisfy first? The whole point of the illustration is to show that in a world

7

of limited resources, a person has to make decisions about how to achieve his goals. He can't achieve all of them at the same time. He has to decide what he needs to do—first, second, and so on, down to a hundred and thirty-fifth or more—and then he has to compare this list with his available resources, including his personal skills and time.

One day he may pick berries. But they don't last forever, and besides, he wants something else to eat. He can climb a tree and pick coconuts, or he can spend several hours to make a sort of poking stick that he can use to knock down fruit or coconuts from trees. But the time he spends locating a suitable stick can't be used to climb trees and get food directly. The point is that he has to give up income (food) in order to get the time to produce or discover capital (the stick).

He may want to go fishing. That means he needs a fishing pole, some line, a hook, and maybe some bait. Or he needs a net. But unless he finds it as a free gift (the ship's warehouse), he has to make it. He can't become too fancy, or else he will die of malnutrition before he finishes the project.

Decisions on Board

Say that he has a pile of goods to take from the ship. He has put together a crude and insecure raft that he can use to float some goods back to shore. The ship is slowly sinking, so he has limited time. A storm is coming up over the horizon. He can't grab everything. What does he take? What is most valuable to him? Obviously, he makes his decision in terms of what he thinks he will need on the island. He tries to estimate what tools will be most valuable, given his new environment.

The value of a tool as far as he is concerned has nothing to do with the money it cost originally. He might be able to pick up a sophisticated clock, or an expensive musical instrument, but he probably won't. He would probably select some inexpensive knives, a mirror (for signaling a passing ship), a barrel (for collecting rain water), and a dozen other simple tools that could mean the difference between life and death.

In short, value is subjective. The economist uses fancy language and says that Crusoe *imputes* value to scarce resources. He decides what it is he wants to accomplish, and then he evaluates the value to him personally of each tool. In other words, the *value of the tool* is completely dependent on the *value of the tool's expected future output*. He mentally calculates the future value of the *expected future* output of each tool, and then he makes judgments about the importance of any given tool in producing this output. Then he calculates how much time he has until the ship sinks, how much weight each tool contributes, how large his raft is, and how choppy the water is. He selects his pile of tools and other goods accordingly.

In other words, he doesn't look to the past in order to evaluate the value to him of any item; he looks to the future. The past is gone. No matter what the goods cost originally, they are valuable now only in terms of what income (including psychic income) they are expected to produce in the future. Whatever they cost in the past is gone forever. Bygones are bygones. The economist calls this the doctrine of *sunk costs*. In the case of Crusoe's ship, that's exactly what they are about to become: sunk. That's why he has to act fast in order to avoid losing everything.

There are objective conditions on the island, and the various tools are also objective, but everything is *evaluated subjectively* by Crusoe. He asks the question, "What value is this item to me?" His assessment is the sole determining factor of what each item is worth. He may make mistakes. He may re-evaluate (re-impute) every item's value later, when he better understands his conditions on the island. He may later wish that he had picked up some other item instead. The point is, it's his decision and his evaluation that count. Because he is all alone, he and he alone determines what everything is worth. He doesn't ask, "How much money did this item cost in the past?" He asks instead, "What goods and benefits will it produce for me in the future?" Then he makes his choices. He *allocates* the scarce means of production. He allocates some to the raft and the rest he leaves on the sinking ship. He loads his top-priority items onto his raft, and floats it back to shore.

The Function of Money

What has money got to do with all this? Absolutely nothing. Crusoe doesn't use money. He simply makes mental estimations of the value of anything in terms of what he thinks it will produce for him in the future. If whatever an item will produce isn't worth very much to him in the future, it won't be worth very much today.

He doesn't ask himself, "I wonder how much money all this cost before it was loaded onto the ship?" Unless he expects to be rescued shortly, thereby enabling him to resell the item, he wouldn't bother with such a question. What does he care how much money any item cost in the past? All that matters is what actual services (non-money income) it will produce for him in the future.

Assume that he has really little hope of being rescued. The ship is sinking. His raft is almost sinking below the water. The storm is coming. He has to get back to shore fast. As he is about to climb off the ship and onto the raft, he remembers that the captain of the ship was rumored to own a chest full of gold coins. Would Crusoe run back to the captain's room to try to find this chest? Even if he had enough time, and even if he really knew where it was, would he drag it to the edge of the ship and try to load it onto the raft? Would he toss the tools into the ocean to make way for a chest of gold coins? Obviously not.

But money is wealth, isn't it? Gold is money. Why wouldn't he sacrifice some inexpensive knives and barrels in order to increase his wealth (money)? The answer is simple: in a one-person environment, *money cannot exist*. It serves no purpose. Crusoe knows that gold is heavy. It displaces tools. It sinks rafts. It's not only useless; it's a liability.

The value of money is determined by what those who value it expect that it will do for them in the future. A lonely man on a deserted island can't think of much that money will do for him in the future. If he remains alone for the rest of his life, there is nothing that money can do for him at all.

So the value of money in this example is zero.

Joseph in Egypt

Now let's take a real historical example, the famine era in Egypt. Joseph had warned the Pharaoh of the famine to come, and for seven years, the Pharaoh's agents had collected one-fifth of the harvest and had stored it in granaries. Then the famine hit. The crops failed. The people of nearby Canaan also suffered. No one had enough food.

"And Joseph gathered up all the money that was found in the land of Egypt and in the land of Canaan, for the grain which they bought; and Joseph brought the money into Pharaoh's house. So when the money failed in the land of Egypt and in the land of Canaan, all the Egyptians came to Joseph and said, 'Give us bread, for why should we die in your presence? For the money has failed' " (Genesis 47:14-15).

What did they mean, "the money has failed"? They meant simply that *compared to the value of life-giving grain*, the money was worth nothing. Why would a man facing starvation want to give up his remaining supply of grain in order to get some money? What good would the money do him? He wanted life, not money, and grain offered life.

Because the money "failed," it had fallen to almost zero value. Thus, in order to buy food, the people had been forced to spend all of their money. Now they were without food or money.

"Then Joseph said, 'Give your livestock, and I will give you bread for your livestock, if the money is gone.' So they brought their livestock to Joseph, and Joseph gave them bread in exchange for the horses, the flocks, the cattle of the herds, and for the donkeys. Thus he fed them with bread in exchange for all their livestock that year." (Genesis 47:16-17).

Were the Egyptians foolish? After all, all those cattle and horses were useful. But animals eat grain. The grain was too valuable during a famine to feed to animals. All that the animals were worth was whatever they would bring as food, ana in Egypt, the meat wouldn't last long. Dead animals in a desert country don't remain valuable very long. Why not trade animals for grain, which survives the heat?

The only reason the Pharaoh had any use for the animals and money is that he knew he had enough food to survive the famine. He knew that it would eventually end. Thus, he would be the owner of all the wealth of Egypt at the end of the famine. For him, the exchange was a good deal, but only because he had the food, and the army to defend it, and he also possessed what he believed to be accurate knowledge concerning when the famine would end. Joseph had told him it would last seven years.

Because he had a surplus of grain beyond mere survival, and because he had "inside information" about the duration of the famine, money and animals were valuable to the Pharaoh, even though they were not valuable to the people. Thus, a voluntary exchange became profitable for both sides. The Pharaoh gave up grain for goods that would again become very valuable in the future. The Egyptians gave up goods worth very little to them in the present in order to get absolutely vital present goods. Each side gave up something less valuable in exchange for something more valuable. Each side improved its economic position. Each side therefore gained in the transaction.

Notice here that we are not dealing with any so-called "equality of exchange." This theory says that people exchange goods only when the goods are of equal value. It is true that in the marketplace, they may be of equal *price*, but they are not of equal value in the minds of the traders. What we are always dealing with in the case of voluntary exchange is *inequality* of exchange. One person wants to possess what the other person has more than he wants to keep what he already has. Because each person evaluates what the other has as more valuable, a voluntary exchange takes place.

Egypt's money failed. In fact, *grain became the new form of money*, although the Bible doesn't say this explicitly. What it says is that everyone was willing to trade whatever he had of *former* value in order to buy food. But if some item is what everyone wants, then we can say that it's the true money.

The Properties of Money

Why would grain have served as money? Because it had the five essential characteristics that all forms of money must have:

1. Divisibility
2. Portability
3. Durability
4. Recognizability
5. Scarcity (high value in relation to volume and weight)

Normally, grain doesn't function as money. Why not? Because of characteristic number five. A particular cup of grain doesn't possess high value, at least not in comparison to a cup of diamonds or a cup of gold coins. The buyer thinks to himself, "There's lots more where that came from." Normally, he's correct; there *is* a lot more grain where that came from. But not during a famine.

Why divisibility? Because you need to count things. Five ounces of *this* for a brand-new *that*. Only three ounces for a used *that*. Both the buyer and the seller need to be able to make a transaction. The seller of the used "that" may want to go out and buy three other used "thats" in order to stay in the "that" business, so he needs some way to divide up the income from the initial sale. This means divisibility: ounces, number of zeroes on a piece of paper, or whatever.

Portability is obvious. It isn't an absolute requirement. I have read that the South Pacific island culture of Yap uses giant stone doughnuts as money. They are too large to move. But they are a sign of wealth, and people are willing to give goods and services to buy them. Actually what are exchanged are ownership certificates of some kind. Normally, however, we prefer something a bit smaller than giant stone doughnuts. When we go to the market, we want to carry money with us. If it can't be carried easily, it probably won't function as money.

Durability is important, too. If your preferred money unit wears out fast or rots, you have to keep replacing it. That means trouble. A barrel of fresh fish in a world without refrigeration won't serve as money. But there are exceptions to the durability rule. Cigarettes aren't durable the way that metal is, but cigarettes have functioned as money in every known modern wartime prison camp. Their high value per unit of weight and volume overcomes the low durability factor. Also, they stay scarce: people keep smoking their capital.

Recognizability is crucial if you're going to persuade anyone to trade with you. If he doesn't see that it's good, old, familiar money, he won't risk giving up ownership of whatever it is that you're trying to buy. If it takes a long time for him to investigate whether or not it's really money, it eats into everyone's valuable time. Investigations aren't free of charge, either. So the costs of exchange go up. People would rather deal with a more familiar money. It's cheaper, faster, and safer.

So what we say is that any object that possesses these five characteristics to one degree or another has the potential of serving a society as money. Some very odd items have served as money historically: sea shells, bear claws, salt, cattle, pieces of paper with politicians' faces on them, and even women. (The problem with women is the divisibility factor: half a woman is worse than no woman at all.)

Money as a Social Product

We have already seen that Robinson Crusoe has no need of money on his island. From there we went to ancient Egypt, and we found that society did initially need money, but when a famine struck, the older forms of money "failed," no longer serving as money. Maybe grain took over as the new money. Or maybe nothing replaced money.

These examples should give us some preliminary ideas about what money is, and how it works. It is used in exchange. Because Robinson Crusoe is all alone, he has no use for money. He doesn't intend to make any voluntary exchanges. Similarly, in a society that is just barely surviving, and almost everyone is a farmer, there will be no reason for money to exist. Nobody buys and sells for money any more. To trade away grain is to trade away life.

They all hang onto every bit of food they grow, and nobody trades very much. They may barter goods and services directly, but they no longer trade by means of money. This indicates a very low amount of trade. So widespread trade ceases. When this happens, money "fails." It dies. It no longer serves society, so it falls into disuse until the crisis is over.

If people don't trade, they can't specialize in production. In the case of Egypt, what had been a rich nation became poor. The Pharaoh was rich, and the people of Egypt survived, but at very high cost: the loss of their freedom. They sold themselves into a form of slavery in order to buy food, for they sold their land and their children's inheritance to Pharaoh (Genesis 47:19-23). That's poverty with a vengeance. But they survived the famine. They bought their lives.

Why does money exist? Because it serves people well. If they want to increase their personal wealth by giving up less valuable items (to them) in order to buy more valuable items (to them), they need trading partners. If I have only cattle to sell, and the person I want to sell to doesn't want cattle, but wants an axe, I have to go find someone who will trade an axe for my cattle, and then I have to try to find the person who wants the axe. I hope and pray he hasn't bought an axe from someone else in the meantime.

But where there's a will, there's a way. Where there is a need in society, men have an incentive to find a way to fill the need. As people trade with one another, they *voluntarily* begin to search out universally desired items in order to hold "for a rainy day." They sell their surplus goods or services for this universally sought-after good. Why? Because they make the assumption that people will want this good tomorrow and next week, too. So if they store up a quantity of this good, they will be able to find people who will be willing to sell them all sorts of goods and services later on. In fact, the owner of this good will be able to change his mind next week about what he wants to buy, and he will still be able to buy it.

In short, and most important, *money is the most marketable commodity in a particular society.* That is the best definition of money that economists have been able to come up with. In Egypt, when the older form of money was no longer marketable, the Bible says that the money failed. "Failed" money is the same as "unmarketable" money. But there is no such thing as unmarketable money. If it's unmarketable, then no one wants it. If no one wants it, it's no longer money.

Money allows us to change our minds inexpensively. It allows us to make mistakes about what we need or want, and we can still recover. Money broadens the number of people who will be willing to sell us what we want. The more people who want money, the more people I will be able to deal with.

Furthermore, money makes it possible for people to establish common prices for most goods and services. I don't have to compute how many axes will buy how many shoes, and then compare shoes with cattle, and sheep with axes, and on and on. All I need to do is to check the newspaper and see all the things I can buy with money. So we all make better decisions because we can *calculate* more effectively. Without money, we can achieve only a primitive economy, because calculating the price of anything, let alone everything, becomes too difficult. In fact, we can define the word "primitive" as "a society without a developed money system."

Money increases the division of labor. It increases our options of buying and selling. It therefore increases our wealth and our freedom of action. It promotes economic growth. And most interesting of all, to achieve all this, the State* doesn't need to produce it. It is a product of individual economic action, not government legislation.

Summary

Robinson Crusoe didn't need money (except perhaps after Friday showed up) because he had no one to trade with. He had to make his calculations of value directly. "I want this most of all, this over here second, that over there third," and so forth. He cal-

---

*I capitalize the word State when referring to civil government in general. I don't capitalize it when I am referring to a United States political jurisdiction called a state.

culated in terms of first, second, third, etc., not by ten units, seven units, five units, etc. He had no units in his head, so he couldn't use them to make comparisons.

In Egypt, the money failed because everyone wanted the same thing, grain, and nobody was willing to give up any grain except the Pharaoh. Trade either ceased or slowed down drastically. Money ceased to serve as a means of trade. The famine made people poor, and as trade was reduced, they became even poorer. The division of labor collapsed. This means that the specialization of production collapsed.

Money is a social phenomenon. It comes into existence because individuals begin to recognize that certain common objects in society are universally sought after. People then sell their goods and services in order to obtain this sought-after good. They store up this commodity because they expect others to sell them what they need in the future. As in the case of Robinson Crusoe on board the ship, people want to own whatever will provide them with income (goods and services) in the future. People make decisions concerning the present and the future. The past is gone forever. Money offers people the widest number of options in the future, so they sell their goods and services in order to buy money in the present.

The principles governing the value of money are these:

1. Economic action begins with an ordered set of wants (first, second, third, etc.).
2. A world of scarcity doesn't permit us to achieve all of our desires at the same time.
3. To increase output, we need capital (tools).
4. We have to sacrifice present income in order to obtain capital.
5. The value of the tool to each person is dependent on the expected value (to him) of the future output of the tool.
6. Value is imputed by a person to goods and services; it is therefore subjective.
7. Past costs are economically irrelevant; present and future income are all that matter.

8. We must allocate our scarce resources rationally in order to achieve our goals.

9. Money doesn't exist if you're all alone.

10. Money is a social phenomenon.

11. The value of money isn't constant (for example, during a famine).

12. There is no "equality of exchange."

13. Money's five characteristics are divisibility, portability, durability, recognizability, and scarcity.

14. Money is the most marketable good.

15. Money increases our options.

16. Money allows us to recover more easily when we have made economic errors.

17. Money increases the division of labor.

18. Money therefore increases our productivity.

19. Money increases our freedom.

20. Money makes possible a highly developed economic calculation.

21. The State doesn't need to create it in order for it to exist.

2

THE ORIGINS OF MONEY

> And the gold of that land [Havilah] is good. Bdellium and the onyx stone are there (Genesis 2:12).

In the second chapter of the Book of Genesis, God, speaking through Moses, saw fit to mention this aspect of the land of Havilah. It was a place where valuable minerals were present. One of these minerals was gold.

We cannot legitimately build a case for a gold standard from this verse. We could as easily build a case for the onyx standard, or a bdellium standard (whatever it was: possibly a white mineral). What we can argue is that Moses knew that people would recognize the importance of the land of Havilah because they would recognize the value of these minerals. One of these minerals was gold.

Why do I stress gold? Historically, gold has served men as the longest-lived form of money on record. Silver, too, has been a popular money metal, but gold is historically king of the money metals. There is no doubt that Moses expected people to recognize the value of gold. We read his words 3,500 years later, and we recognize the importance of the land of Havilah. If we could locate it on a map, there would be as wild a gold rush today as there would have been in Moses' day. No one thinks to himself, "I wonder what gold was?"

Money: Past, Present, and Future
You may remember from the previous chapter that money appears in a society when individuals begin to recognize that a particular commodity is becoming widely accepted in exchange.

People want to be able to buy what they want tomorrow or next week or next year. They aren't really sure which economic goods will be in demand then, so they seek out one good which will probably be in heavy demand. They can buy units of this good now, put them away, and then buy what other goods or services they want later on. In short, money is the most marketable commodity. It is marketable because people expect it to be *valuable in the future*.

This isn't too difficult to understand. But it raises a problem. The unit we call money is valuable today. We have to sell goods or services in order to buy it. In other words, money has already established itself as the common unit of economic calculation. My labor is worth a tenth of a unit per hour. A brain surgeon's labor is worth a full unit. A new car is worth ten units. Money has exchange value today. If it didn't, it wouldn't be money. We have all learned about money's value in our daily affairs. We are familiar with it.

How do we know what it's worth today? We know what it was worth yesterday. We have a historical record for its purchasing power. If we didn't know anything about money's value in the past, we would not accept it as a unit of account today. If it has no history, why should anyone expect it to have a future? But if people don't expect it to have a future, it can't serve as money.

So here is the key question: How did money originate? If it has to have a history in order to have present value, how did it come into existence in the first place? Are we confronting a chicken-and-egg problem?

This was the intellectual problem faced by one of the greatest economists of all time, Ludwig von Mises, an Austrian scholar. In his book, *The Theory of Money and Credit* (1912), he offered a solution to this important question. Money, he argued, came into existence because in earlier times, it was valued for other properties. He thought that gold was probably one of the earliest forms of money—not a unique observation, certainly. Before it functioned as money, it must have served other purposes. Perhaps it was used as jewelry. Possibly it was used as ornamentation. We know that many religions have used gold as part of their ornaments. It is shining, lovely to look at, and widely recognized.

Gold in the Bible

Anyone familiar with the Bible would recognize the accuracy of Mises' theory. Abraham's servant gave Rebekah gifts in order to lure her into marriage with Isaac. These gifts included jewelry made of silver and gold (Genesis 24:53). When the Israelites fled Egypt, they were told by God to collect "spoils" as repayment for their long enslavement: jewels of gold and silver (Exodus 3:22).

God warned the Israelites not to make gods of gold or silver to worship (Exodus 20:23), indicating that this was a common form of idolatry in pagan lands. But his tabernacle was to be filled with gold ornaments (Exodus 25, 26, 28, 37, 39). So was the temple (1 Kings 6, 7:48-51, 10). As a possible (though not conclusive) argument, we can compare the shining brilliance of gold with the glory cloud of God (Ezekiel 1:4). It is not surprising that men adopted gold in religious worship, and then in ornamentation and jewelry.

Gold has the five characteristics of money: divisibility, durability, transportability, recognizability, and scarcity (in relation to weight and volume). It is uniquely divisible. It can be cut with an iron or steel knife in its pure form. It can be hammered incredibly fine. It is uniquely durable; only an acid, aqua regia, destroys it. It is easily transported and easily hidden. It is instantly recognizable. As for its scarcity, throughout history it has been exceedingly scarce in relation to other metals. Men have searched for it for as long as we have records.

We can understand how it was that gold came into common use as a form of money. People recognized its beauty, and its close connection with the gods. Men who are made in God's image understandably desire to collect gold for themselves. If God wants gold in his places of worship, why shouldn't people want gold to adorn themselves?

God described His love of Israel by describing figuratively what He had done for His people. Like a bride, Israel had been given ornaments, bracelets, chains around her neck, a jewel in her forehead and earrings. "Thus you were adorned with gold and silver, and your clothing was of fine linen, silk, and embroidered cloth. You ate pastry of fine flour, honey, and oil. You were exceedingly beautiful, and succeeded to royalty" (Ezekiel 16:13).

The Most Marketable Commodity

Gold has been the most marketable commodity for thousands of years. A seller of gold has not had to stand in the streets desperately begging people to consider buying his gold. If anything, he has needed bodyguards to keep people from stealing his gold.

Understand from the beginning that the State was not necessarily a part of the development of gold and silver as money. There is nothing in the Bible that indicates that gold and silver became money metals because Abraham, Moses, David, or any other political leader announced one afternoon: "From now on, gold is money!" The State only affirmed what the market had created. It collected taxes in gold and silver. It thereby acknowledged the value which market forces had imputed to gold and silver. But the State didn't create money.

Notice also that if Mises' argument is correct concerning the development of money, the original money units must have been commodity-based. If the unit of account (for example, gold) must have come into popular use because of its past value, at some point we must conclude that it was valuable as a commodity for some benefit that it brought besides serving as the most marketable commodity: money. Money had to start somewhere. It had to originate sometime. Before it was money, it must have been a commodity.

In short, money was not originally a piece of paper with a politician's picture on it.

Money and Taxes

There is no doubt that the State can strongly influence the continuation of one or more metals as an acceptable unit of money. All the State has to do is to announce: "From now on, everyone will be required to pay his taxes in a particular unit of account." After all, taxes are an expense. There is no escape from death and taxes. (But, fortunately, the death rate doesn't go up every time Congress meets.) The State has power. If it says that people must pay their taxes in a particular unit of account, there will be strong incentives for people to store up this form of money.

Still, the State doesn't have an absolutely free hand in selecting this unit of account. If it imposes on people a legal obligation to pay what the people cannot actually gain access to, there will be no revenues. In the Middle Ages, for example, there were no gold coins in circulation in Western Europe until the mid-1200's. There was no way that a king or emperor could compel people to pay gold in the year 1100 or 900, because his subjects couldn't get any gold. They had nothing valued by the East (Byzantium, the Eastern Roman Empire) that could be exchanged for gold.

The Bible is clear: taxes to the State were paid both "in kind" (a tithe of actual agricultural production: 1 Samuel 8:14-15) and "in cash," meaning silver. A head tax was required when the nation was numbered immediately before a military conflict (Exodus 30:12-14)—the only time that it was lawful for the State to conduct a census, as King David later learned (2 Samuel 24:1-17). Solomon collected 666 talents of gold (1 Kings 10:14), presumably from taxes, gifts from other nations, and from the sale of any agricultural produce he collected. (We aren't told where he got this huge quantity of gold.)

Tribute in silver and gold was paid to a militarily victorious State. There were incidents when Israel had to pay such tribute (2 Kings 15:19; 23:33) and also when foreign nations paid tribute to Israel (2 Chronicles 27:5).

The State also hired military forces with gold (2 Chronicles 25:6). Thus, taxes came into the treasury in the form of silver and gold, but then expenditures by the State came back out in the same form. There is no doubt that this process made silver and gold the familiar forms of money in the ancient Near East. There are plenty of examples in ancient records from other Near East societies that they asked for tribute in gold and silver. It was the common currency of the ancient world.

What must be fully understood is that there were no coins in this era. Coins didn't appear in the world until about 600 years before Christ. This would have been about the time that Judah fell to the invading Babylonians, quite late in Hebrew history. So there was no system of State money with the monarch's picture or other symbols on the metal bars, or if there was, no examples of such markings have survived. It is reasonably certain that the State did not manufacture the metallic bars in ancient Israel.

This means that the State did not originate money. A theoretical model ("blueprint") for the origin of money doesn't need to include any reference to the State. The State's decision about what to tax clearly had an influence on the kind of money people accepted, but that decision was tied to the existing kind of money that was already being used by the people. In short, "If it ain't being used, you can't tax it."

This is very important to understand from the beginning. There are many economists who rely heavily on the idea that the State was the source of money originally, and that whatever the State designates as money *is* money. This explanation is Biblically incorrect, historically incorrect, and logically incorrect. Money is the product of individuals who make decisions to buy and sell. If individuals refuse to use what the State designates as money, it isn't money. If the State refuses to use what the market has designated as money, it can't collect taxes or buy people's services and goods. The State can influence the value of a particular kind of money, or the popularity of that money, for the State is a big buyer and seller of goods and services. But the State cannot autonomously create money and impose it on the market if market participants don't want to use it.

No Committee Needed

It is difficult for many people to understand that the free market operates rationally, even though there is no committee of expert planners or politicians to tell the market what to produce. People find it difficult to believe that God's world is a world in which individual people, responsible before God and their fellow men, go about their daily business, making decisions, planning for the future, and focusing their attention on their own personal and family needs, and out of all this hustling and bustling, pushing and shoving, comes the most productive economy in the history of man.

Christians can believe that the world is orderly because it was created by God. The Bible teaches that God is sovereign, but men are fully responsible for their actions. As they interact with one another, they learn things. They find out what they must offer to other people in order to buy what they want. They also find out what other people are willing and able to offer them for the things that they presently own. Market competition is a form of *exchanging information*. Free market activity can be described as a *process of discovery*.

We don't need a committee to tell us what we need to do to satisfy other buyers. In fact, a committee cannot possibly know all the things that we know as individuals, taken as a group. What we learn we can put to profitable use later on.

This spread of knowledge is made much easier by the existence of an agreed-upon currency unit. I don't mean that we all sat down and agreed to use it. I mean that people learned that other people will usually accept a particular currency in exchange for goods and services. As this learning process continues, certain currency units become familiar. It's always easier for us to deal with each other if "the rules of the game" are known in advance. The currency unit is the most important single source of information concerning the state of the actual conditions of supply and demand.

Who decides which currency unit is acceptable? Originally, the people did who entered into agreements with each other about buying and selling. They learned what was good for them, and the rest of us have continued to learn. A currency unit becomes familiar. We get into the habit of calculating the price of everything in terms of this familiar unit. It saves us time and effort when we can mentally estimate: "Let's see, I can buy three of these, but only two of those, or five of yours, or eight of hers. Which do I want more?"

Do you want a committee to set prices? Do you think a committee can sit down and decide what everything should cost in relation to everything else? Will a committee be an intelligent, reliable economic representative of all of us? Most of us know the answer most of the time: *no*.

Why then would a committee do such a terrific job in deciding how much money to create or destroy? If the committee can't set prices, why should it be allowed to control the supply of money in which all prices are quoted? Why should we trust a committee in money questions when the committee didn't invent money, and when the committee can't know enough to tell all of us what we *really* need or should *really* pay?

Here's another question. How do we know that the committee will act only in behalf of us citizens? How can we be sure that the committee won't start fooling around with the money supply in order to feather its own economic nest? Monopolies are always dangerous. Why should some government committee have a legal monopoly over money? No committee invented money. No committee showed the rest of us how to use money. Why should any committee possess absolute control over money, now that the rest of us have decided on what kind of money we want?

Summary

Money is a very important social institution. It was no more invented by a government than language was. True, the government can influence money in the same way that it can influence language, but it is not the source of money's origins. It cannot impose its monetary decisions on the public unless people decide that the government is doing the right thing. If people change their minds later on, they can change the government or voluntarily, transaction by transaction, change over to a new form of money.

Historically, people have voluntarily selected gold as the common medium of exchange. Silver has also been widely acceptable, all over the world. No government legislated this; people simply came to use these two metals in their economic transactions.

Why do people select a particular form of money? Because they learn from experience that other people *usually* accept this monetary unit in exchange. We can make better predictions and plans about the future when we discover that other people generally have accepted a certain currency unit in the past. What people habitually do they tend to keep on doing. They have a right to change their minds, but it's easier not to, at least most of the time. Thus, money allows us to gain access in the future to the goods and services we think we will want, or even to new ones that we haven't thought about yet.

Thus, historically it was the free market which determined what was acceptable to people for their economic activities. It happened to be gold and silver, but other commodities have sometimes been used widely. The point is, people *voluntarily* selected what they wanted to use as money. They did not need a committee to make this decision for them.

The principles of the origins of money are therefore these:

1. The Bible doesn't say that people should be required to use gold and silver as money.

2. The Bible does indicate that people in Biblical times came to use gold and silver as money.

3. Money will be selected because people expect others to use it in the future.

4. To establish what money is worth today, we need information about what it was worth yesterday.

5. Tracing this principle backward, we conclude that the money commodity must have been used for something else originally.

6. Gold and silver were used as jewelry and ornaments.

7. The beauty of gold and silver probably had something to do with their popularity.

8. The symbolic shining of gold may have been connected in people's minds with God's glory.

9. The metallurgical properties of gold make it highly suitable as money (the five characteristics).

10. Money is the most marketable commodity.

11. The State can influence the continued use of a monetary unit by taxing and spending in terms of that unit.

12. Some economists argue that money is what the State says it is.

13. The Biblical evidence points to the conclusion that money is what the market says it is.

14. A committee didn't originate money.

15. A committee isn't needed to maintain money.

16. A monopoly over money is a dangerous grant of power by the State.

3

MAINTAINING HONEST MONEY

You shall do no injustice in judgment, in measurement of length, weight, or volume. You shall have just balances, just weights, a just ephah, and a just hin: I am the Lord your God, who brought you out of the land of Egypt (Leviticus 19:35-36).

It's not necessary to get into a debate over just exactly what units of measurement an "ephah" and a "hin" were. The point is clear enough: once defined, they could not be changed by individuals in the marketplace.

Who defined them? That isn't said. Not the Hebrew civil government, in all likelihood, because it was being set up at the time the law was announced. Like the widespread use of gold and silver, certain weights and measures had also come into widespread use on a voluntary basis. The important thing was not that the civil government make its definitions "scientific"; the important thing was for the civil government to enforce a *consistent* standard.

It should be noted that God immediately provides the reason for this commandment: He is the One who brought them out of Egyptian bondage. He is the Lord, the sovereign master of the universe. He is the deliverer of Israel. To avoid being placed in bondage once again, they had to discipline themselves. First, they had to discipline themselves by means of honest weights and measures. Second, they had to discipline themselves by means of God's comprehensive moral law.

We cannot do without discipline. It is never a question of "discipline or no discipline." It is always a question of *whose* discipline.

29

Will we be disciplined by ourselves, as individuals under God's law? Will we be disciplined by God directly (for example, when He sends a plague on us, as He did several times in the Old Testament)? Or will we be disciplined by the State? In our day, State tyranny is the most common alternative to self-discipline.

Without self-discipline under God's revealed laws, there can be no freedom. False weights and measures lead to unrighteousness. People who sell items to the public must be sure that they avoid giving less than what is expected—revealed on the scales—through tampering with the physical standards. In short, tampering with the society's *physical standards* is a sign that men have already tampered with the society's *moral standards*.

Market Scales

When a person in Old Testament times (indeed, up until relatively modern times) went to market in order to buy something, he brought with him something valuable to exchange. In barter societies, he would bring some home-grown or home-made item for sale. He would try to exchange it for someone else's home-grown item, or manufactured item.

If a man brought something that would require weighing (for example, a sheep) and wanted to trade it for some other item that required weighing (for example, a sack of wheat), the question of accurate scales was less important. If something was underweighed for the "seller," it was equally underweighed for the "buyer." (Remember, both parties are buyers and sellers simultaneously: one buys wheat and sells a sheep, while the other buys a sheep and sells wheat.) Dishonest weights would be those in which the professional seller—the man who could afford the scales—tampered with the weights in one half of the transaction. Tampering in half the transaction probably isn't easy.

When people started bringing metals to market in order to buy consumer goods, it became easier for sellers to use dishonest scales. The metal bar or item would normally be measured in small units of weight ("ounces"), or even smaller ("grams"), in the case of gold. But the item being sold for money would, if sold by weight, probably require much heavier units ("pounds"). The man with the scales could cheat the buyer by lightening up the money metal scale, while making heavier the product scale.

Thus, once money metals came into widespread use, as they would in an advancing, high division of labor economy, the opportunities to commit fraud increased drastically.

The Seller's Advantage

The seller in the marketplace normally has an advantage over the buyers. He understands his trade, especially scales. It is easier for the professional seller to tamper with the scales than it is for the buyer to tamper with the coins. This is not a universal rule, however. Coin clipping is an ancient practice. People would shave a bit of the gold off the rim. This is why coins have those little ridges around them: to reduce theft (a legacy of the days when coins were made of valuable metals). I have heard that the Chinese immigrants in California in the gold rush days would place several gold coins in a small sack and have old people or young children in the family shake the sack, until gold flakes would rub off. Then they would collect the dust from the sack.

There is another odd example from United States history. In the late 1800's, during the "wild west" era, a famous crooked cattleman named Dan Drew herded his cattle for days without allowing them access to water. Then, just before he sold them, he would let them drink their fill. He would then take them to the stockyards and sell them. This became known as "watering the stock." The same term was later applied to a similar immoral practice by corporations. Corporate officers would print up huge quantities of ownership certificates (stock) and sell them whenever some outside group would try to take over the company by buying up 51% of the outstanding shares. The buyers wound up with shares of depreciated value—"watered down stock."

On the whole, though, the professional produce seller with the scales is more likely to cheat than the seller of goods. It is he who is *normally* the focus of attention by the civil government. On the other hand, it is easiest to check him, for he operates in a public place.

Perhaps even more important, the seller of produce has competitors. Buyers catch on when they are being cheated, if they have access to a rival. The competitors have an economic incentive to warn the buyers, or warn the civil government, about the fraud at any particular shop. Thus, *market competition* tends to pressure produce sellers to stay honest, at least within the generally accepted "permissible range" of the free market.

Scales of Justice

God links the ownership of scales with His own sovereignty. The man who owns the scales is a judge. God judges men in terms of moral standards. He is a Judge with the scales of justice. When the evil Babylonian king Belshazzar was having his great feast, in the midst of a military siege by the Medo-Persians, the hand of God wrote the famous words on the wall: "MENE, MENE, TEKEL, UPHARSIN." The king called Daniel to translate, and Daniel did so: "MENE: God has numbered your kingdom, and finished it; TEKEL: You have been weighed in the balances, and found wanting" (Daniel 5:25-27).

Weighed in the balance: this is symbolic of God's final judgment. Therefore, the man who controls the "scales" of civil justice is a judge. So is the man who controls the actual weights and measures in the marketplace.

If a man misuses his position and cheats people, he is thereby testifying falsely to the character of God. He is saying, in effect, that God cares nothing for justice, that He tips the balance, that He cheats mankind for His own ends. *This is precisely what Satan implies about God's role as Judge.* It is false witness against God. Thus, God warns men that they must use honest weights and measures, for He is the sovereign God who delivered them out of bondage. He implies that He has the power *to deliver them back into bondage* if they cheat in this very special area of economics.

Honest Metal Money

What was money in ancient Israel in the days before the Babylonian captivity? It would have been any item that people voluntarily accepted in exchange for goods and services. The only monetary units identified in the Bible relating to money were the shekel and the talent. These were *units of weight*. In principle, though the Bible doesn't specify this, they were also units of fineness. ("Fineness" refers to the percentage of pure gold or silver in the total weight of the coin.) We conclude this because of the fact that base (cheaper) metals can be melted in when the smelter is pouring the metal into the molds. Weight was not enough; there had to be a particular fineness.

Years ago, when I was a boy, I visited Juarez, Mexico with my family. I saw an old woman sitting in front of a stall in a large market. Someone handed her a coin. She stuck the coin into her mouth and bit it. I couldn't figure it out. My mother told me it was her way of testing the coin. If it wasn't soft enough for her teeth to leave a mark, it wasn't the proper weight of the precious metal.

An ingot or coin of a specific size, assuming it's well known, is known by sellers to weigh a certain amount. By measuring the ingot or coin, and then by weighing it, the expert can determine whether it's of the standard fineness (the proper mixture of a base metal for hardness and a precious metal for value). I own a simple, inexpensive set of weights and measures that measure the more common gold coins.

The weights and measures for the ingot of gold or silver is the professional seller's defense against fraud. The scales for produce are the buyer's protection against fraud.

The Bible lays down the rule of honest weights and measures. To tamper with the scales is a moral evil. It is theft through fraud. Someone trusts the seller, and the seller misuses this trust. It is easier to cheat a trusting person because the latter isn't watching every move of the seller. Thus, tampering with the scales is a major sin. When sellers get away with it because the authorities look the other way, honest, trusting people lose, while crooked dealers win. This reverses God's standards for dominion, namely, dominion by ethical behavior. Furthermore, it reduces the efficiency of the market, for buyers have to devote extra time and trouble in testing sellers. God will not tolerate such behavior indefinitely.

One reason why gold and silver came into widespread use in the ancient world was that they could be tested by sellers of goods and services. Today, a seller of goods (buyer of money) can use simple tools, if necessary, to determine the reliability of a particular ingot or coin. He could test the ingots in the ancient world, too, using similar simple tools. Because gold and silver were recognized, and because standards of shape and weight made it possible for people to test the full weight (precious metal content) of the ingots, these two metals could more easily function as the most marketable commodities in society.

Honest money is easy to define in the context of a pure precious-metals ingot or coin economy. An ingot or coin contains a specific quantity of gold or silver of a known fineness. In the case of the famous U.S. "double eagle," the $20 gold piece, the coin weighed 1.075 troy ounces (the standard unit for measuring gold), with .967 ounces of pure gold and the rest copper, for hardness.

For greatest ease of use, an ingot would be stamped with some familiar mark or company, so that the user would know that smelter or firm stands behind the honesty of the weights and measures. The coin or ingot in a literate society would announce its weight and fineness of the metal (such as one ounce, .999 fine). Perhaps the traditional names of national currencies might be retained on the coins — "dollar," "yen," "peso," etc. — but to reduce confusion to a minimum, it would be better to have no name attached. It would simply be a one-ounce gold coin. With or without a familiar name, the coin when originally produced would contain exactly what it says concerning the precious metal.

To tamper with either the weight or the fineness of the coin would be like pouring water into the ground meat at the supermarket. It would be fraudulent: the attempt to get something for nothing.

Honest Paper Money

Coins and ingots are heavy and bulky. It should be obvious why people prefer paper money. It fits into a wallet or purse. It's flat. It's easily recognizable. Paper can be printed to represent any number of currency units: 1, 5, 10, 20, 50, 100, and so forth.

The key word is *represent*. The paper money, to remain honest, must be issued by the money-issuer on a strict one-to-one basis. If it announces that it represents a one-ounce gold coin, .999 pure, then the issuer must have that one-ounce coin in reserve, ready to be redeemed by anyone who walks in and presents the piece of paper.

To issue a piece of paper that serves as an IOU for precious metals without having 100% of the promised metal in reserve is fraudulent. It is theft. It is a form of tampering with weights and measures.

How would such a system work? The coin owner might deposit his coins at a warehouse. He wants his coins kept safely. He pays a fee for the safekeeping, the same way we rent safety deposit boxes at our bank. The warehouse issues a receipt. Since the receipt promises to pay the bearer a specific amount of coins, or ingots, on demand, the paper circulates as if it were gold, assuming that everyone knows and trusts the warehouse that issued the receipt.

Warning: whenever someone promises to store your precious metals for free, watch out. You never get something for nothing. Either there is a hidden payment, or else there is fraud. Any system of paper money or credit that doesn't somewhere involve a fee for storage is unquestionably and inevitably fraudulent. Keep looking until you identify the form of fraud.

The paper certificate is a *metal substitute*, sometimes called a *money substitute*. But it isn't a money substitute; it really is money, *if the metal on reserve is regarded as money.* Its value in exchange rises or falls according to the exchange value of the money metal in reserve.

The big problem is counterfeiting. It is a lot easier to counterfeit a piece of paper than it is to counterfeit a gold coin. A counterfeit coin is easier to detect. It can be weighed. A piece of paper looks just like other pieces of paper. So issuers take care to identify pieces of paper by serial numbers, or special water marks, or by using special paper that is easy to identify by the public.

A counterfeiter is clearly a thief when he prints up false

warehouse receipts. Some company is required by law to redeem the paper receipts by paying out the specified quantity and fineness of gold or silver. To issue phony receipts places the issuer at risk. Or, if the company should go bankrupt and be unable to redeem the notes, it places at risk the last person who accepted the receipt at face value. He goes to get his gold, and the issuing company has gone bankrupt. He is stuck with a worthless warehouse receipt, whereas the counterfeiter has bought valuable goods and services. The loser (among others) is the last guy to get stuck with the bad receipt when the bad news is made public. Unquestionably, counterfeiting is a form of theft.

One way to protect users from counterfeit bills is for the bank to allow the depositor to write receipts for the deposited coins whenever he makes a transaction. This way, the user has to sign his name at the time of purchase. He writes checks (warehouse receipts) until he runs out of coins in reserve. Then he stops, unless he is a thief, or he makes a mistake (and pays a penalty to the bank), or he has made prior arrangements with the warehouse to "cover" his checks with *extra gold which is held in reserve* — gold that has no warehouse receipts issued against it — for this purpose by the warehouse firm.

This is why checks are money, *if the money metal backing them up is money.* They are metal substitutes. An honest check is simply another form of warehouse receipt.

A credit card is also money, *if the metal backing up the credit card is money.* It, too, is a metal substitute. An honest credit card is simply another form of warehouse receipt.

We could add all sorts of examples to this line of reasoning, but by now you have the idea. The key is the honesty of the warehouse firm. If it issues no more receipts than it has gold or silver in reserve to redeem the receipts, then the receipts can legitimately serve as forms of money.

If a warehouse company issues more receipts to valuable money metals than it has metals on reserve, then it has violated the law against false weights and measures. The difference is that it is harder to detect a false (unbacked) warehouse receipt than it is to detect a counterfeit coin not containing the stated amount of gold or silver. The coin can be measured and weighed; the paper bill can't. But the principle is the same in both cases: counterfeit coins or counterfeit warehouse receipts.

Summary

The principle of honest money is quite easy to understand. You deliver what you say you're delivering. If you promise to give an ounce of gold, .999 fine, to a seller, then that's what you deliver. He can make an estimation of how much that ounce of gold is worth to him, and if he decides that he wants the gold more than he wants what he has offered for sale, then you get the item, and he gets the gold.

If either of the parties tampers with the scales, or in any way substitutes something less valuable than what he has agreed to deliver, then he has committed a sin. This sin is an attack on God's principles of justice and man's social peace. The sinner must make double restitution (Exodus 22:11-12): the return of the value stolen, plus a 100% penalty.

The law regarding honest weights and measures is obviously a specific (case-law) application of the eighth commandment: "You shall not steal" (Exodus 20:15). But because God is a Judge, and because the symbolism of His perfect judgment is the scales, honest weights and measures become a theological issue as well as an economic issue. To tamper with the scales is to defy God in a unique way. It is to assert that man, the law breaker, being made in God's image, reflects a God who is equally a lawbreaker.

Honest money is an economic application of the law against false weights and measures. Because money in the Bible is metallic, any tampering with the content of the precious metal is the equivalent of tampering with the scales. Counterfeiting coins is illegal. So is the counterfeiting of paper money: creating more warehouse receipts for precious metal than there is precious metal on reserve for future redemption.

We find the principles of honest money involve the following:

1. The prevailing definitions of measurement must be observed in all our dealings with one another.

2. The civil government need not be the originator of these standards, though it is supposed to certify them.

3. The goal is consistency of use.

4. The God who requires honest measures is the same God who delivered Israel from bondage.

5. Violating these physical standards is the equivalent of violating God's moral standards.

6. The professional seller in the marketplace has more opportunities to tamper with the scales.

7. Market competitors monitor each other, thereby reducing the extent of tampering.

8. God's activities as Judge symbolically undergird the law of honest weights and measures.

9. Money in ancient Israel consisted of gold and silver in familiar sizes and shapes.

10. When the civil magistrate refuses to enforce honest weights and measures, evil people temporarily prosper at the expense of honest people. This reverses God's standards of dominion.

11. Widespread dishonest weights also increases everyone's transaction costs (costs of exchanging): time involved in checking scales.

11. Paper money represents specific quantities of gold or silver (or whatever money unit which is common).

13. Any issuing of warehouse receipts to money constitutes a violation of the law prohibiting dishonest weights and measures.

14. Issuing more receipts than there is metal to redeem them is a form of counterfeiting.

15. Paper bills, checks, and credit cards are all forms of metal substitutes; they are all true money.

16. Whenever some agency promises to create a paper money system that doesn't require storage fees for money metals, it's making a fraudulent offer. You don't get something for nothing.

4

DEBASING THE CURRENCY

Your silver has become dross, your wine mixed with water
(Isaiah 1:22).

The prophet Isaiah came before the nation of Judah, the
Southern Kingdom of the divided nation of Israel, sometime
around the year 750 B.C. He began his ministry with a condemna
tion of the spiritual condition of the people, from the man in the
street to the rulers.

The Old Testament prophets didn't just talk about the internal
mental state of the people. They believed in what the Bible
teaches, that the heart of a people is reflected in their actions.
Almost eight centuries later, Jesus said: "Even so, every good tree
bears good fruit, but a bad tree bears bad fruit. A good tree cannot bear bad fruit, nor can a bad tree bear good fruit. Every tree
that does not bear good fruit is cut down and thrown into the fire.
Therefore by their fruits you shall know them" (Matthew 7:17-20).

Jesus also said, "A good man out of the good treasure of his
heart brings forth good; and an evil man out of the evil treasure of
his heart brings forth evil . . ." (Luke 6:45a).

Isaiah was saying exactly what Jesus said so many years later.
The people were corrupt in their hearts. He used the imagery of
dross. What is dross? It is cheap or "base" metal. It is unfavorably
compared with precious metals, silver and gold. It can be re-
moved from the precious metal only by melting down the ingot
and purging out the base metal, either by heat or by chemical re-
action. This, too, is a familiar Bible image: purging away dross
by placing the metal into a hot fire.

39

God spoke to the prophet Ezekiel, who wrote over a hundred and fifty years after Isaiah: "Son of man, the house of Israel has become dross to Me; they are all bronze, tin, iron, and lead, in the midst of a furnace; they have become dross from silver" (Ezekiel 22:18).

This same imagery is found in the New Testament, regarding the final judgment of God. The apostle Paul wrote concerning Christians who are judged on the day of the Lord: "Each one's work will become manifest; for the Day will declare it, because it will be revealed by fire; and the fire will test each one's work, of what sort it is. If anyone's work which he has built on it [the foundation of Jesus Christ: verse 11] endures, he will receive a reward. If anyone's work is burned, he will suffer loss: but he himself will be saved, yet so as through fire" (1 Corinthians 3:13-15).

Those who rely of the work of Christ at Calvary are Christians. If their life's work is dross and is "burned up," they will survive the ordeal, but without rewards. Those who don't trust in Christ's perfect (zero-dross) work at Calvary are doomed to wind up as "permanent dross" in eternal judgment. The apostle John saw their fearful destiny in his God-given vision of the future: "And anyone not found written in the Book of Life was cast into the lake of fire" (Revelation 20:15).

The Old Testament prophets understood that sin served as dross in Israel. They knew that if people did not "purge away" their spiritual dross voluntarily through personal moral reform, to be followed by political, economic, and institutional moral reform, then God would purge the whole nation. There would be war, or plague, or famine. God will not tolerate moral dross indefinitely. Isaiah announced the warning of God: "I will turn my hand against you, and thoroughly purge away your dross, and take away all your alloy" (Isaiah 1:25).

Moral Evil Produces Public Evil

The prophets were God's prosecuting attorneys. God brought them before Israel with His case against the people. God had set forth His law at Mt. Sinai, and He had placed them under a covenant. Obedience to God's covenant brings *external, visible blessings*, He promised (Deuteronomy 28:1-14), while disobedience brings *external, visible cursings* (Deuteronomy 28:15-68). The list of cursings is much longer than the list of blessings. God wanted them to know just how serious He is about obedience to His law — *eternally* serious.

As an "officer of God's court," the prophets brought God's covenantal lawsuit against Israel and Judah. But to make a case, the prophets had to have evidence. It is not enough in God's earthly law court that people are *suspected* of harboring evil thoughts. It is not enough to convict someone in God's earthly court of *bad intentions*. There must be public evidence of a crime. "Whoever is worthy of death shall be put to death on the testimony of two or three witnesses, but he shall not be put to death on the testimony of one witness" (Deuteronomy 17:6).

This is why God sent many prophets to bring charges against Israel. In Isaiah's day, there also appeared Hosea (Hosea 1:1 has the same list of kings as that in Isaiah 1:1), Amos (Amos 1:1), and about a generation later, Micah (Micah 1:1). They all brought the same message of God's anger and coming judgment.

What was the public evidence? First, Isaiah pointed to the false judgment by the rulers. "How the faithful city has become a harlot! It was full of justice; righteousness lodged in it, but now murderers" (1:21). Second, he pointed to the dross metal in the silver, and the water in the wine (1:22). Third, he returned to the theme of corrupt judgment: "Your princes are rebellious, And companions of thieves; Everyone loves bribes, And follows after rewards. They do not defend the fatherless, Nor does the cause of the widow come before them" (1:23).

Notice that the sins listed by Isaiah are quite specific: murderers in the capital city (evidence of a breakdown of law and order), debased commodities being sold as high quality, and false judgment by bribe-seeking, gift-seeking judges. Even before he began to talk about the spiritual sins of the people (dross in their hearts), he spoke about the visible sins of the rulers. The rulers were visibly corrupt, indicating that *the people were also corrupt*. The corrupt leaders of Judah were true *representatives of the people*.

I worked on Capitol Hill as an assistant to a United States congressman in 1976. The crime rate in Washington, D.C. was so bad even then that Congress employed its own police force to patrol the few square blocks where Congress is located: over a thousand officers, a police force larger than the entire U.S. border patrol guarding the U.S.-Mexico border.

Within a few minutes' taxi ride from the Capitol, there were street corners on which prostitutes attracted (and still attract) their clients. The parks at night were (and are) filled with male homosexual prostitutes. More abortions are performed in Washington, D.C. each year than there are live births.

When I was working there, two of the most powerful congressmen had their careers destroyed by revelations concerning their adulterous affairs with young women. One of these women, who was on the congressmen's paid staff as a secretary, wrote a bestselling book about her activities. The second congressman later admitted his long-time problem with alcoholism and did not run for re-election.

But the sign of this corruption at the highest levels of government had been visible since 1965. It was in that year that the United States abandoned its silver currency and substituted a "pure dross standard" of silvery (but not actual silver) plated copper coins. Not only had the silver become partially dross; it had become entirely dross. The government plated the coins for tradition's sake, but there was no more precious metal in them.

Gold coins had been illegal in the U.S. since 1934.

The point which must be understood is that there is a relationship between the moral corruption of a nation's citizens, the moral corruption of their political representatives, and the debasement of the currency. The prophet Isaiah did not simply bring a complaint against exclusively internal spiritual sins; he brought God's covenant lawsuit against the leaders for their specific public sins. They were no longer enforcing God's law as His representatives to the people. Instead, as representatives of a corrupt population, they were enforcing the people's God-defying standards on the defenseless.

Weights and Measures

We have already seen in Chapter Three that God requires the civil government to enforce predictable standards of weight and measure. This makes it easier for people to make voluntary economic transactions in a free market. Not only do we say, as buyers and sellers, "What you see is what you get," we also implicitly say, "What *I say* you are getting you will get." More specifically, "What *my scale* says you are getting is what you will get."

Our scales are symbols of God's justice. If we rig our scales to cheat our customers, we are implicitly saying either that God doesn't care (because He is also at heart a cheater) or that God can't do anything about it (meaning that He isn't really God). We are saying that God as Judge of all mankind is a liar. He isn't really a Judge. Therefore, if we can get the earthly judges to "look the other way," we can continue to cheat our customers.

Corrupt businessmen want to deal with civil officers who are equally corrupt. They are willing to pay bribes to get them to "look the other way," to get them to "turn a deaf ear" to those weak people who will be cheated by corrupt scales. This was Isaiah's accusation against the leaders: they were bribe-seekers, people who did not hear the widow's plea.

But they were something else. They were also men who refused to prosecute those who tampered with false scales. Remember, the State in this era did not issue coins. Coins were invented about a century later. There is no indication that the State even certified the weight and fineness of any ingots in circulation as money. But the State could prosecute fraud. The authorities could prosecute anyone who was passing dross-filled silver or gold bars as if they were high quality (normal market standard).

Centuries later, when officials learned about the "wonders" of debased money, they made the State the monopolist over money. Instead of serving God by enforcing laws against debased money, politicians took the profits for the State. They "eliminated the middlemen." They stopped taking bribes from the corrupt money-manufacturers and started stealing from the public directly. One of the main reasons that the Roman Empire fell into the hands of the Christians around 320 A.D. is that the pagan emperors had destroyed the Roman coinage system. Nobody trusted the money, so nobody trusted the State.

The Process of Debasement

Why would any private producer of silver ingots want to debase his product? Because he could get more *short-run* profits by doing so.

Say that you are a corrupt expert at smelting metals. This skilled trade was a near-secret trade in the ancient world. A secret guild controlled mining and smelting in many cultures. Not many people knew the secrets. This made corruption easier, whenever the guild decided to produce short-term profits for its members.

The smelter could do the following. He had molds into which he poured molten metal. He could pour in pure silver, but silver was in short supply. This was why it was a precious metal. It was a lot cheaper to buy tin. So the cheater would melt down some tin, and then pour a little tin into the formerly pure liquid silver.

Who would know? The ingot would still look shiny. It would look like silver. How many people would own accurate measures and scales to detect the shift in weight produced by the tin? Hardly anyone.

The silver producer could sell the debased silver in exchange for scarce goods and services. But by adding cheap metals (dross), he could continue to buy as many scarce goods and services as he had been able to buy the day before with pure silver. People trusted him. They wouldn't measure and weigh his ingots. They wouldn't insult him in this way.

But what if the authorities found out? He could bribe them. Only if the bribe was as valuable as the profits on the deception would he really worry.

It was a simple scheme. Just pour "a little" tin, or other cheap metal, into the molten silver, pour the molten metal into an ingot, and there was instant profit.

What is his profit? The extra silver he has left after the tin has replaced silver in the ingot. But understand: this extra silver can be translated into profit only by "spending it into circulation"—in other words, by selling it in exchange for additional goods and services.

Who Wins, Who Loses?

Our world is a world of scarcity. It is also a world of God-imposed law. The rule says: "You never get something for nothing, except as a gift." This testifies to God's mercy in redeeming us: salvation is a gift: "For by grace you have been saved through faith, and that not of yourselves: it is the gift of God" (Ephesians 2:8). But this gift had to be paid for: Jesus died on the cross to meet God's stiff requirements against sin. "But God demonstrates His own love toward us, in that while we were still sinners, Christ died for us" (Romans 5:8).

So if someone is able to win by cheating, someone else becomes a loser. It is not a question of everyone winning because there has been new wealth created in the economy. It is profit based on deception. No new wealth has been created. Someone has to lose.

The person who buys the "silver" ingot uses it for something. Perhaps he makes an ornament. He sells the ornament, or barters with it. But the buyer gets stuck with an ornament which is overpriced. Why? Because the original cheater can collect his profit only by selling the extra silver into the market. Someone will make more ornaments (or whatever) with this extra silver. The supply of "silver" ornaments goes up; therefore, the value (price) of the existing supply of "silver" ornaments will drop. The early buyer has overpaid.

What if the cheater just produces ingots, and "spends them into circulation"? He trades the debased ingots for something he wants. If whoever sells him what he wants then turns around and sells the newly produced debased ingot for whatever he wants, he will not be hurt economically. The secret is this: *sell the ingot before a lot more phony silver ingots hit the market*. In other words, "get while the getting is good." Or "take the money and run"—run to the nearest store and buy goods with it.

Those who are hurt are those who hold onto these debased ingots too long. As more and more of them flood the market—remember, the only way for the cheaters to collect their profits is to spend the extra silver—one of two things happens. First, if the dross in the new ingots is undetectable, the market price of all silver ingots will fall: more supply, lower price per ingot. Second, if the dross-filled ingots are detectable (inexpensively), then the price of the phony silver ingots will drop in relation to pure silver ingots. This means that there will be two separate price-quote systems in the economy: a pure silver price per good or service, and a dross-filled silver price per good or service.

In either case, the person who is stuck with a pile of dross-filled ingots will lose when prices rise. He sold goods and services at yesterday's lower price level, but he will buy his goods and services at today's higher price level, or perhaps at tomorrow's even higher price level.

Thus, the winners are those who get access to the phony money early, *and spend it fast*. The losers are those who get access to the phony money later, after prices in general have risen. Worse, what about the people on fixed money incomes, who don't see their incomes rise at all, but who now face higher prices?

Who are these people likely to be? Pensioners. Small businesses that are barely making money. In short, *widows*: the very people that Isaiah said were being harmed by false judgment. They were to be protected, and to fail to do so was a sign of sin within the nation, but especially among the rulers: "You shall not afflict any widow or fatherless child. If you afflict them in any way, and they cry at all unto Me, I will surely hear their cry; and My wrath will become hot, and I will kill you with the sword; your wives shall be widows, and your children fatherless" (Exodus 22:22-24).

Isaiah was threatening them with just such military judgment by God. This is why it is ridiculous to argue that Isaiah was not talking about the specific sin of monetary debasement, but only of a strictly "spiritual analogy." He was talking about *corrupt metal* which was itself a reflection of *corrupt hearts*. He was talking about both forms of corruption.

Summary

The prophets came before Israel with a covenant lawsuit from God. They warned the people that if they refused to repent, from the lowest worker to the king himself, that God would bring judgment against them. He would "purge their dross." This judgment would be as visible as their sins. This judgment would not be limited to "internal" crises: psychological fears, and so forth. His judgment would be both internal and external, just as their sins were both internal and external.

One sign of their sinful condition was their corrupt silver. Their money was corrupt, dross-filled. Their money reflected their moral condition. It testified against them publicly. They had debased their money because they had debased their morals. The two practices went together.

Historically, nations that are marked by honest money do not fall to external enemies. Wars that are begun with honest money are fought with dishonest money: debasement on a massive scale. Both sides do it, but the truth is still the truth: the loser will not be found with clean hands, monetarily speaking.

Civilizations fall when they become morally corrupt. One sign of this corruption in virtually all known instances is debased money. When a society finds that its rulers have debased the currency unit, the people receive a warning: the rulers are corrupt, and if the people continue to support these rulers, then they, too, are corrupt.

And in modern times, civil governments have the full support of their people for at least "limited inflation," meaning "a little corruption" of the money supply.

We have learned the following lessons from Isaiah's critique of Judah:

1. A corrupt tree brings forth corrupt fruit.
2. The people were morally corrupt.
3. God promised to "purge" them because of their sins.

4. A sign of this moral corruption was the debased condition of their money.

5. Their sins were therefore not simply "internal" sins.

6. Corrupt citizens prefer corrupt rulers.

7. The capital city was corrupt: murderers lived there, the money was corrupt, and false judgment was common.

8. In short, Isaiah listed specific sins as specific violations of specific laws.

9. The corruption of their silver was a violation against God's law regarding false weights and measures.

10. The profit from debasing silver can come only when the supply of debased ingots increases.

11. The corrupt metal producer produces corrupt metal.

12. He buys more goods and services than would otherwise have been possible.

13. The holders of the debased ingots will eventually suffer losses, as prices of other goods and services rise.

14. The secret of success in a time of corrupt money is rapidly to sell the money for goods and services.

15. Those who are on fixed money incomes are hurt: widows.

16. The treatment of the weak (widows) is a sign of a nation's commitment to God's law.

5

THE CONTAGION OF INFLATION

Your silver has become dross, Your wine mixed with water (Isaiah 1:22).

In Chapter Four, I focused on the actual process of debasing a precious metal currency. I discussed Isaiah's accusation against the rulers that they were not enforcing God's law, and this was reflected in the corruption of the nation's silver. He used this to point out the spiritual rebellion of all the people, from the highest to the lowest. The corruption had spread from top to bottom, and back again.

If moral corruption is widespread, then there is no more characteristic sin than monetary debasement, for money is the common medium of exchange. Everyone in an advanced economy uses it. Thus, if the money is corrupt, everyone will eventually recognize this. Corrupt money testifies to the corruption of the producers of money, the defenders of money, and the users of money. Corrupt money testifies to corrupt people.

Where we find debased money without widespread protests, we also find debased people. The people of Judah could see the debased money. This is why Isaiah called it to their attention. He knew that they would recognize the truth of what he said concerning their corrupt money; he used this to call their attention to their corrupt hearts. He started with the simple, and worked toward the more subtle. (Jesus did the same thing when he used parables to make His points: "pocketbook" parables and agricultural parables.)

Once the process of moral debasement begins to spread, it is very hard to stop it. People must stand in principle against this spreading moral corruption. The more that people see that corruption seems to profit people, at least in the short run, the more difficult it is to get people to change. The corruption is contagious, almost like a disease. But it isn't a disease; it's a moral condition. It may be accompanied by disease—venereal diseases, for example —but it isn't itself a disease.

Moral corruption is sometimes spread by passive acceptance, but only because God's representatives, the priests of society, have been silent in warning the people about their moral obligation to challenge such practices by forthright, active resistance. Also, such "passive, ill-informed acceptance" of somewhat obscure sins (for example, monetary debasement) is always accompanied by practices that *are* recognized by the simplest people as corrupt, but which they actively pursue anyway. Pornography is a good example in our day; so is abortion.

Wine Mixed With Water

It was not simply that Judah's silver had become dross. Their wine had also become adulterated.

Consider the winemaker. He spent a lot of time growing, caring for, and harvesting his grapes. It took time for the fermentation process to produce wine. These retarding factors reduced the available quantity of wine. Thus, for people to buy it, they had to pay a higher price than they would have been forced by competition to pay if there had been abundant supplies of comparable-quality wine.

By the way, we should not argue that the high cost of wine production is what produced the high prices. This has cause and effect backward. What we should recognize is that all those buyers competed against each other to buy the wine. Their willingness to pay for it is what lured producers to stop producing other products and start producing wine. Buyers determined the price of wine by competitive bidding; the producers didn't force the buyers to buy it. In short, *consumers set prices, not producers*. If producers set prices too high, many consumers won't buy; they will buy something else instead, and then the high-price producers have to lower prices or suffer losses.

It is obvious that if good wine were easy to produce in huge quantities, consumers would not have to bid so much money to buy the wine. But it isn't cheap to produce in large quantities, so they do have to pay high prices.

Now, let's return to the problem that faced the prophet Isaiah: the moral corruption of the people. It was not just the silversmiths who were corrupt. It was the winemakers, too. It was everyone.

How did the winemaker practice his corruption? By a process almost identical to that of the silversmith: *debasement*. The silversmith was pouring cheaper base metals into the molten silver, and calling the product silver. This was precisely the process of the corrupt winemaker. He was pouring "debased wine" (water) into the pure wine, and calling it pure wine.

How could he make his profit? The same way the corrupt silversmith made his. He would displace pure wine when he poured in the water. This displaced wine could then be used to pour into other wineskins along with more water. Then he could take, say, 20% more wineskins full of "wine" to market and sell them. Presto: a 20% profit, *at least initially.*

He was trading on his own former reputation. Before, he had produced a high-quality product (just as the silversmith had formerly produced). *People trusted his products because they trusted his morals.* So he could take advantage of this trust by pouring water in the wine. He was simply imitating the silversmith.

But moral corruption being what it is, it never stays in one place. It gets worse. So more and more water would wind up in the wine, just as more and more dross would wind up in the silver. Pretty soon, everyone would begin to see that a particular silversmith's silver was mostly dross, and a particular winemaker's wine was mostly water. At that point, people would stop doing business with these corrupt people, or else start offering them fewer valuable goods and services in exchange.

Unless. . . .

Unless the *existing* silversmiths were acting as a giant monopoly to debase the silver uniformly (a cartel). Unless the *existing* winemakers were doing the same thing. Unless they controlled the markets (with the cooperation of the rulers) to keep out competitors who were willing and able to offer consumers high quality silver or wine.

With government controls against honest newcomers, it would have been possible for corrupt sellers to maintain their corrupt practices and not lose their markets to honest newcomers. But this would have required coercion against newcomers, either directly (privately hired thugs) or indirectly (thugs hired by the government).

This was the very essence of economic oppression in Biblical times. It still is. When corrupt producers capture the government in order to keep out honest producers, the losers are consumers. They are the ones whose interests are hurt, not just the interests of honest producers who are kept out.

Widespread economic oppression always requires the consent of the governors. In God's world, it also requires the consent of the governed. God brings oppressors against those who practice oppression privately and who want to practice it without threat of judgment by the civil government. God hears the cries of the afflicted, and brings judgment against the oppressors (Exodus 22:22-24).

The Bible says that specific corrupt practices are like yeast (what the Bible calls "leaven"): they corrupt the whole loaf. But, on the other hand, honest dealing is also like yeast; it, too, can spread to the whole loaf. What determines which yeast is more powerful in any particular society? The hearts of the people. They will choose which kind of yeast they prefer, corrupt or incorrupt. In Judah, they had chosen corrupt practices.

Gresham's Law

Back in the late 1500's, an official in Queen Elizabeth's court, Sir Thomas Gresham, made a famous observation. He said that "bad money drives good money out of circulation." In short, debased money drives honest money out of circulation.

But if God's law really does rule the world, how can this be true? How is it that something bad (corrupt, phony, debased money) can drive good money (pure gold or silver) out of circulation? Is there something corrupt about market competition? Why should the bad product defeat the good product in a competitive free market?

Economists finally figured out the answer. Something was missing from Gresham's analysis. The bad money drives out the good money *only when the government says the two are equal in value, and enforces this decision with the threat of punishment.*

If I have a silver coin that will buy a loaf of bread, and I also have a phony, silver-looking coin that has only half the silver, the latter coin should buy only half a loaf of bread. But what if the government says the two coins are of equal value? Which coin will I spend on the loaf of bread, the full silver coin or the phony? I will spend the phony coin and hoard the full silver one, or trade the full silver coin to someone who wants to give me (perhaps illegally) three-quarters of a loaf of bread for it. (The bread seller will keep an extra quarter loaf—or whatever—as his profit, to compensate him for trouble and risk.)

So Gresham's law should read: "The coin that is *artificially overvalued* by the government will drive out of legal, visible circulation the coin which is *artificially undervalued* by the government."

But this artificial price which is set by the government *isn't* a free market price. It's a *form of coercion*. It's a lie which is enforced as if it were truth. It's another example of the government's violation of God's law concerning *weights and measures*.

The Spread of Corrupt Products

Let us consider a society in which the rulers have established a fixed price which equates honest money (full-weight of gold or silver) with dishonest money (partially gold or silver, or even zero-content of gold or silver). The government lies, and it enforces that lie on everyone.

We are rational people. We don't want to spend a full silver coin on a product which says "for sale for one silver coin." We would much rather spend the common coin which lies, which says "pure silver," but which is in fact only half silver. We will hoard the full silver coin for a better deal at a later time.

What does the businessman do? He knows he will not be getting full silver coins into his till that day. He knows his customers will spend the half-silver coins. Now what should he do:

1. Continue to sell his product for "one silver coin," when he knows that he will receive only half-silver coins?

2. Double his price to two silver coins, in order to get the same amount of silver per item sold?

3. Debase his product with cheaper quality materials, but maintain the fiction that each unit is worth one silver coin—the real, old-fashioned, true silver coin?

Consider the consequences to him of each of the three possible decisions:

1. Same price, same product: he gets stuck with phony coins. He is selling his product at 50% of what it was worth before the phony coins started circulating.

2. Doubled price, same product: he risks losing sales. Maybe his competitors will take the third approach, and debase their products. His customers, not being experts at quality controls, may not recognize this. He loses business.

3. Same price, reduced quality: his customers are initially defrauded (until they figure out the new rules). He sells fraudulent "high-quality" goods at the familiar (pre-debased money) price.

You can understand how tempting the third decision is. The government is not enforcing the law of honest weights and measures against corrupt silversmiths. Silversmiths who don't practice corruption cannot get the government to step in and stop the deception of their competitors. Their competitors make more profits, and the honest ones eventually go out of business, or begin to imitate the corrupt silversmiths.

Once the silversmiths are all (or mostly) corrupt because of the corruption of the rulers, the other producers face a problem as individuals. Should they raise prices? Should they instead cut profit margins but try to sell high-quality goods at the older, familiar price? Or should they follow the lead of the corrupt silversmiths, and start debasing the quality of their products?

Isaiah's condemnation of Judah indicates that the winemakers had fallen into the same corruption as the silversmiths. They were pouring water into the wine.

Step by step, the debasement of money provides incentives in the short run for deception. The sellers are tempted to deceive the public. But remember, *the public wants to be deceived*. The public wants to believe in something for nothing. The public is crooked, too.

Something for Nothing

The worker who is employed by the silversmith says to himself, "I want a raise. I see that my boss is corrupting the silver, and he is pocketing the profits. I want 'a piece of the action.' He can afford to give me a raise." To keep his employee quiet, the silversmith gives him a raise. The worker now gets paid in extra quantities of the debased silver. He, too, can rush out and spend it on goods and services at *yesterday's prices*. He, too, has "won." He, too, has been corrupted.

What does the person do who sells something to the silversmith's employee? He makes more money. Business has picked up! He orders more goods to sell to the employee next payday. And what does his employee think? "My boss is getting rich by selling goods to these silversmith workers. I want my piece of the action." So he asks for a raise, and gets it.

And so it goes, all the way through the economy. Everyone just loves having more money. Everyone loves becoming a bigger spender. Everyone seems to have gotten something for nothing.

Guess what starts happening to prices? Right: they start going up. So what do consumers do? Some pay more for the things they buy. (That's why prices go up.) But others start looking for bargains: sellers who are "stupid," who keep selling goods at older, pre-inflationary prices. Buyers seek bargains, meaning older-priced goods and services. They want something (discounts) for nothing (lots of debased new money jingling in their pockets).

So corrupt wine sellers accommodate corrupt buyers. "Yes, sir, a brand-new, 100% top-quality item at low, old prices!" Meanwhile, they have poured water into their wine. So do a lot of other sellers.

The quality of many products starts going down. Prices stay artificially low, because in principle people are violating the principle of honest weights and measures—all through the society. "Yes, you get ten yards of 100% silk at last year's low prices." It's a lie. Either the silk isn't 100% silk, or it's an inferior quality silk, or it's actually seven yards because the seller has substituted a false measure.

Price Controls

But what if the government steps in and tells all the other sellers *except* the silversmiths to maintain the old standards of quality? Then either prices will rise, or else the amount consumers can buy at the old prices will be reduced, or else quality will drop.

But what if the government passes a law against raising prices? This means that sellers can't cut the amount sold. What then? Quality will have to drop.

What if the government passes another law, making it illegal to cut quality? Then many sellers will go out of business, and consumers will not be able to buy all the goods they want.

Meanwhile, risk-oriented producers will start selling their goods in the free market, meaning an unregulated market, meaning the *black market*.

(I hate to use the term "black market." I prefer to use the term "alternative zones of supply.")

If the silversmiths alone are allowed to debase their product —money—and the government passes laws against price rises or quality cutting, the law-abiding consumer and the law-abiding producer will be ruined.

Summary

In short, if there is any tampering with the monetary unit, and the government allows such fraud to continue, the whole economy is threatened with a progressive debasement. It is not simply the monetary unit that will be debased, but also many other products. Any seller or producer who finds that his consumers are unwilling to accept price increases is forced to consider adopting the same corrupt practices as the silversmiths, just to stay in business.

Thus, a debased currency is like a giant engine of economic corruption. Where the rulers allow, not to mention promote, this sort of debasement, the whole society is brought under the temptation of adopting corrupt practices. Because money is the universally used medium of exchange, debasement of money is the most efficient "yeast of corruption" that an economy faces. If governments allow this debasement, to say nothing of getting a monopoly over money and then beginning the process of debasement, the spread of immorality speeds up. Every economic enterprise is tempted to imitate the corrupters in order to stay in business.

Something for nothing in the field of monetary policy eventually leads to disaster. God will not be mocked.

Thus, the process of monetary debasement causes a string of undesirable, yet tempting effects. The people of Judah were in sin.

1. People could see the debasement of silver, yet there was no opposition.

2. The rulers were corrupt in allowing the debasement of silver.

3. The spread of monetary corruption was not merely passive; evil was widespread in Judah.

4. (Now let's talk about today.) High quality goods normally cost more to produce than low quality goods.

5. Producers begin to imitate the corrupt practices of money debasers.

6. Continued monetary debasement requires the cooperation of government, meaning coercion (direct or indirect) against honest money producers.

7. Evil and good both spread like yeast (what the Bible calls leaven).

8. Bad money drives good money out of circulation *only* when the government equates the two by law.

9. The public thinks it benefits from the inflation, at least at first.

10. The public wants to fool sellers into selling at "discount" (honest money) prices.

11. Sellers fool the public by cutting quality and offering "discount" prices.

12. The corruption spreads from employers to employees.

13. Government-legislated price controls are in fact "people controls." They control the decisions of people, not prices as such.

14. Government price controls reduce people's wealth by destroying the free market.

15. The "black market" is simply the product of people who are trying to escape dishonest money in a world of price controls.

6

WHEN THE STATE MONOPOLIZES MONEY

"Show me the tax money." So they brought Him a denarius. And He said to them, "Whose image and inscription is this?" They said to Him, "Caesar's." And He said to them, "Render therefore to Caesar the things that are Caesar's, and to God the things that are God's" (Matthew 22:19-21).

By the days of Jesus, rulers had learned the wonders of issuing money. No longer was money the product of silversmiths or goldsmiths. No longer did private individuals have the legal right to issue ingots or other easily recognized units made with precious metal. The State had made money a monopoly.

There were many reasons for this. Let's begin with the key fact in this famous confrontation between Jesus and the Pharisees: the face and the inscription. The coin was a Roman silver denarius. It was specifically a tax coin, a coin for paying tribute to Rome.

Now, why would the questioners ask him about the lawfulness of a Roman tax? To tempt Him. Either He would say that it was unlawful to pay the tax, and incur the wrath of the Roman authorities in Jerusalem, or He would say to pay it, and incur the wrath of the multitudes who followed Him. So He turned the tables on them—figuratively, this time. He had already turned the tables on them in the temple (Matthew 21:12).

What kind of coin did they bring Him? A tribute coin. So they possessed a tribute coin? Of course. This meant that because of the realities of Roman power, they had already made their own decision to use coins as currency that were tax coins. They were the beneficiaries of a widely respected coinage system which had

59

been imposed by a foreign ruler. If they profited from the system, why shouldn't they pay taxes to support the system? End of argument.

We can learn a lot by a study of Roman coinage. The Roman Empire was a religious organization—all ancient societies were. (So are all modern societies, but most of them disguise this fact.) Increasingly, the emperors were regarded as gods, especially in the eastern half of the Roman Empire. The coins were used as political devices. In an illiterate world, the pictures on the coins announced religious messages, and therefore political messages.

Tiberius Caesar's picture was on the denarius that they handed to Jesus. Tiberius issued only three types of denarii during his reign, and by far the most widely circulated had his face on one side, adorned with a laurel wreath, a sign of his divinity. The inscription read, "Emperor Tiberius august Son of the august God," referring to Caesar Augustus, the father who had adopted him.

On the back of the coin, his mother appears, seated on a throne of the gods. In her right hand she holds an Olympian scepter, and in her left hand is an olive branch, a symbol of peace. As Professor Stauffer comments concerning the coin: "It is a symbol of power. For it is the instrument of Roman imperial policy."

Roman coins from Augustus on, announced divine emperors, saviors of the world. Yet by the year 300, the coins were worthless, price controls had been imposed, and the empire was an economic catastrophe. The more the coins promised deliverance, the worse they became. The silver was taken out of them, and cheap copper was substituted. Professor Stauffer's book, *Christ and the Caesars* (1955), tells the story of the collapse of the pagan Roman Empire through a study of its progressively debased coinage. As the Empire collapsed, so did its coinage.

A Sign of Sovereignty

Political rulers learned very early just how powerful coins could be in serving as symbols of political and religious authority. They could serve as unification devices, just as flags serve modern men. The users were reminded constantly of the source of the coins (the State) and the person who made the State possible (the political-religious leader).

It is not surprising that the first coins ever issued were issued in order to strengthen the State. While Greek coins in the ancient world were in part used to expand commerce, historians are now generally agreed that political motives were equally important as economic motives. The right to issue coinage was a sign of a city-state's political and legal independence. In other words, the State's officials saw coins as an effective means of strengthening citizens' loyalty to the existing government.

But the symbolic importance of coins was only the beginning. The State could use coins as a means of collecting taxes. If the State issued precious metal coins, it could collect coins as taxes. This made it easier to keep tax records, and politicians always like to simplify tax collecting! The State could buy goods and services, including the services of armies, if it had coins.

Where could the State get the precious metals? From mines, or from successful warfare, or from taxing businessmen who were involved in trade. Once the State sanctioned money, it would have led to an increase in demand for *certified money*. After all, the State collected its taxes with its own money. This would have created demand for money just in itself.

Eventually, the politicians learned about the short-term benefits of debasing the currency. They learned quite early, in fact. When the State took in gold and silver, it then issued coins that were pure. But as time went on, and people became accustomed to the coins, the old debasement trick became too tempting for politicians to resist.

People don't like to pay taxes. They never have. Politicians love to spend money. They always have. So politicians long ago figured out a way to increase spending without increasing direct tax collections. If they just took out some of that molten gold or silver, and poured in some cheaper metal, they could produce more coins with the extra gold or silver. You have heard all this before. (Take a "silver" coin—ha, ha—out of your pocket. You have in your hand tangible proof that politicians haven't changed over the last two thousand years or so.)

The government then spends these extra coins into circulation. It makes little difference in the long run whether it's the government or a private silversmith who does this. The result is more coins in circulation. Prices will eventually go up. The trick is to spend the debased money before everyone else catches on and hikes selling prices.

There is a new problem, however. The people may trust the State more than they trust private silversmiths. They think that the State is honest. In the old days, they thought the State was divine. Thus, when the State starts producing debased money, it threatens people's confidence in law and order. In the ancient world, it made people doubt the honesty of the gods.

We are back to God's laws regarding honest weights and measures. If God is the Judge, then His lawful representatives in the civil government should not cheat. To cheat here is to call into question the *reliability* and the *integrity* of God.

The State may be able to get away with the debasement process longer, since people trust the State. But coins are coins, and if more of them are coming into circulation, people are building up a supply in reserve. Why not spend some of the extra ones? As they are spent, prices begin to climb, compared to last year's prices, which were produced by an economy with fewer coins in circulation.

Ultimately, it doesn't matter who produces the coins. People will respond to the new conditions of the supply and demand for money. If there is a greater supply of money, the price (exchange value) of the money will drop. Holders of cash will be hurt.

A New Form of Debasement

The trouble with money metals from the politicians' point of view is the very measurable character of metal. If a user can measure it and weigh it, he can tell if someone has added a cheaper metal to the precious metal. The coin's weight will change. It also starts to change color as more and more base metals are added. Then everyone finds out about the corruption.

People lose faith in the issuer of the coins.

But paper money overcomes this inherent weakness. One piece of paper looks like any other piece of paper. They all weigh the same. How can the user determine which piece of paper is the phony? He can't.

How does the State get people to accept pieces of paper as money? By making them convertible on demand for silver or gold. Then the State just starts issuing more paper notes than it has gold in reserve. Most people don't catch on. They accept the State's paper as if it were honest money. After all, these are our leaders. They wouldn't cheat us.

Yes they will . . . if they think they can get away with it. They can, too. They already have: in the United States in 1933 (gold) and 1967 (silver).

As more and more pieces of paper come into circulation, the price of goods starts to rise. This includes the price of gold or silver. Now, if a piece of paper called "one dollar" entitles the bearer to collect an ounce of silver, but the printing of paper money raises the price of silver to "two dollars," it pays the person who owns the piece of paper to go the treasury and get an ounce of silver with his paper dollar.

Guess what he then does with the ounce of silver? He takes it to a free market silver dealer and sells it for two dollars. Then he takes two dollars to the treasury and gets two ounces of silver. Then he sells it to the public for four dollars. Then he. . . .

You get the picture. The treasury will run out of silver. In fact, it will run out a long time before the free market price hits two dollars an ounce. It will run out by the time it hits a dollar and ten cents, probably.

So the politicians either have to stop printing more paper money, or else they have to "shut the window" on people who want to exchange dollars for silver.

This is what they did in the United States in 1967. The following year, the price of silver doubled.

Why didn't they stop printing paper dollars? Don't be silly. If they had stopped creating money, they would have had to raise taxes (unpopular) or cut back government spending (even more unpopular). So they printed money instead. So prices of goods and services more than tripled, 1967-85.

Will the Public Revolt?

Not very often. The public decides that paper money is money, not pieces of shiny metal. If paper is acceptable by the store down the street, then who cares? Who cares if prices go up, year after year? What's "a little" price inflation? We're all doing better, aren't we?

The trouble is, we are all thinking short term. We forget what happens to the value of our money when its purchasing power erodes year after year (that is, prices keep going up). What happens if you retire and are forced to live on a fixed money income? Look at the table on page 65. See what happens to what your money is worth at various rates of price inflation.

Pick a year. See what happens to your income at various rates of inflation. It isn't comforting.

"Inflation can't hurt anyone too badly" is a delusion of fully employed younger workers. It can hurt everyone who isn't staying ahead of it with pay increases, and I mean *after-tax* pay increases.

Higher Tax Brackets

That's another reason why governments like inflation. Governments since the era of World War I have convinced voters to violate the Biblical principle of the tithe, and impose higher rates of taxation on people with higher incomes. This is done in the name of a higher morality. It is done in the name of justice.

At first, only rich people are supposed to be taxed at these higher rates. That's what the politicians promise. Cross their hearts and hope to die. In 1913, the year the income tax was passed in the United States, the tax rates began at 1% and went as high as 7%. The 1% rate was applied to all income over $20,000 a year, and the 7% tax was on all income over $500,000 a year. This was in an era in which the average family earned about $1,000 a year. Almost nobody got taxed for about four years.

**PURCHASING POWER OF $100 OF FIXED PENSION BENEFITS
UNDER VARIOUS RATES OF INFLATION**

Years after retire-ment						Inflation Rate							
	3%	4%	5%	6%	7%	8%	9%	10%	11%	12%	13%	14%	15%
1	97	96	95	94	93	93	92	91	90	89	88	88	87
2	94	93	91	89	88	85	84	83	81	80	78	77	76
3	92	89	86	84	81	79	77	75	74	71	69	68	66
4	88	85	82	79	76	74	71	68	66	64	61	59	57
5	86	82	78	75	71	68	65	62	60	57	54	52	50
6	84	79	75	70	67	63	60	56	53	51	48	46	43
7	81	76	71	67	62	58	55	51	48	45	42	40	38
8	79	73	68	63	58	54	50	47	43	40	38	35	33
9	77	70	65	59	54	50	46	42	39	36	33	31	28
10	75	68	61	56	51	46	42	39	35	32	29	27	25
11	72	65	58	53	47	43	39	35	32	29	26	24	22
12	70	63	56	50	44	40	36	32	29	27	23	21	19
13	68	60	53	47	41	37	33	29	26	23	20	18	16
14	66	58	51	44	39	34	30	26	23	20	18	16	14
15	64	56	48	42	36	32	27	24	21	18	16	14	12
16	63	53	46	40	34	29	25	22	19	16	14	12	11
17	61	51	44	37	32	27	23	20	17	15	13	11	9
18	59	50	41	35	30	25	21	18	15	13	11	9	8
19	57	47	40	33	27	23	19	16	14	12	10	8	7
20	55	46	38	31	26	21	18	15	12	10	9	7	6

Then, in 1917, the bottom bracket was dropped from $20,000 a year to $2,000. The politicians swept a lot more people into the net. And look at what they did to the top brackets: 1913-15: **7%**;

1916, **15%**; 1917, **67%**, 1918, **77%**. In short, they changed the rules. They always do.

Here was their plan: lower the level of taxable income, and increase the rate of taxation in every bracket. Next, inflate the money supply, so that everyone is pushed into higher and higher taxable brackets. The higher your *money* income, the larger the percentage of your income gets collected by the State.

The "graduated" income tax (also called the "progressive" income tax) was recommended by Karl Marx, the founder of Communism, in his 1848 book, the *Communist Manifesto*. He understood that such a tax system would help to destroy private property. He forgot to mention that it would place a major temptation in front of politicians to inflate the currency, increase everyone's *money* income, and push everyone into higher tax brackets.

The lure of greater tax revenues from a graduated income tax makes inflating the currency look too productive. It makes the immorality of changing weights and measures look like a good idea. It makes the destruction of people's economic futures too popular. The government begins to inflate, and almost never in history has the process stopped until the value of the currency falls to zero. It may take a hundred years, but at the end, the people lose what they had needed: a reliable, generally predictable monetary system.

Inflation is an invisible tax. Instead of taxing people directly, the politicians fool people. They increase government spending but they don't collect enough tax revenues to pay for it. So they print up the money to make up the difference and spend it into circulation. The victims (people on fixed money incomes who face rising prices) seldom know who it is who ruined them. They blame "speculators" and "price gougers," not the politicians.

But eventually everyone learns who did it to them. They read a book like this one. They get angry. Inflation of the currency is a good way to create a revolution. The politicians figure this out way too late.

Two Kinds of Counterfeiters

The private counterfeiter prints up currency and spends it into circulation. The government counterfeiter prints up money and spends it into circulation.

Private counterfeiting raises prices if enough counterfeiters do it fast enough and long enough. Government counterfeiting raises prices if the government does it fast enough and long enough.

The private counterfeiter doesn't agree to deliver a specified weight and fineness of gold or silver to the person who "cashes in" his paper note. The government counterfeiter does promise to cash in gold or silver for paper, but eventually he breaks his promise.

The public doesn't trust private counterfeit money. The public *does* trust government counterfeit money, at least for a long time, until people's trust is totally betrayed (mass inflation).

What is the difference *in principle* between private counterfeiting and government counterfeiting? None.

What is the difference *economically*? Only the beneficiaries: private counterfeiters who buy up goods and services, or politicians who buy up goods, services, and votes.

What is the difference *politically*? Private counterfeiters betray people's trust in criminals. Government counterfeiters betray people's trust in the government.

If government counterfeiters and private counterfeiters both issue paper and call it money, then on what *legal* basis can the government prosecute counterfeiters. The only thing I can think of is that it's a violation of the government's trademark laws.

Summary

From about 600 to 500 B.C., governments began issuing gold, silver, gold-silver, and copper coins. This became an aspect of the authority of civil government. Cities (which were city-states) claimed a political monopoly over money. So did the Roman Empire several centuries later.

The coinage system was both a religious and a political phenomenon. It was also economic. As people began to use the coins of a particular government because of the familiarity of the coins, a temptation was placed in front of the government: to debase the currency. The government could buy extra goods and services for itself—initially, before prices started to rise—by spending new (debased) money into circulation. All it had to do was mix dross metals in with the precious metals. In short, coins made it easier for corrupt governments to steal from trusting citizens.

Eventually, people caught on, and people started asking higher prices. After all, the economy is a giant auction, and if people are given more money by the State, they can afford to bid prices higher than before they got access to the new money.

Rising prices eventually destroy people's confidence in the money system. This loss of confidence eventually reflects in their loss of confidence in the State. It is the State's responsibility to protect the integrity of the money, because the State is supposed to enforce honest weights and measures.

But who can enforce honest weights and measures regarding money if the enforcers — politicians and rulers — are profiting from the cheating? That is the problem that no society has ever been able to solve. Government money eventually becomes corrupt money.

It boils down to this: it is cheaper to print a piece of paper with some dead politician's picture on it than it is to mine gold two miles beneath the earth. Being cheaper, it becomes too great a temptation for politicians to resist in a crisis, or even in peaceful times. They are unrestricted by the geology of gold mining. All they need is paper and ink.

When the voters have larceny in their hearts ("something for nothing" from the government), they eventually get stuck with *nothing for something*: they sell their goods and services to the government, and get depreciating paper money in return. When they try to spend it, they find out they have been robbed by the robbers they elected. God will not be mocked.

All this happens because people accept it when the State grants itself a monopoly over money. The politicians violate Biblical principles, but nobody protests. The State's money system is eventually destroyed. So are those who have become dependent on it.

The State step by step violates these principles:

  1. The State at most is supposed to certify the honesty of money: weight and fineness.

2. The State then violates the principle of economic freedom: allowing people to buy and sell on their own terms: it makes private coins illegal.

3. The State claims for itself an economic monopoly that it cannot be trusted to possess.

4. The State in the ancient world used the coinage to propagandize the public (false religion).

5. The State misuses the trust of the people.

6. The State becomes an official debaser of the metal coinage: adding cheap metal ("dross") to the precious metal.

7. These new, "dross" coins add to the number of monetary units in use.

8. People then bid up the price of goods and services, since they have more money to spend.

9. Price inflation begins to erode people's faith in the money.

10. The modern State uses paper money to hide, and then speed up, the debasement process.

11. The State has imposed an invisible tax: inflation.

12. Economically and morally, there is no difference between private counterfeiting and public counterfeiting.

13. Politically, there is a difference: the public loses faith in the law.

7

BIBLICAL BANKING

"Therefore you ought to have deposited my money to the bankers [money exchangers], and at my coming I would have received back my own with interest" (Matthew 25:27).

The translators of the King James Version of the Bible (1611) translated the Greek word *toku* as "usury." But it doesn't mean usury in the Greek; it means "interest." This is how modern translations translate it. There is a difference between usury and interest.

How did the King James scholars make such an error? Because they assumed that the concept of interest in the Bible always means usury. The Hebrew word "usury" was a term of criticism. Usury referred only to interest taken from a poor fellow believer, in other words, interest secured from a *charitable* loan. Such usury is prohibited by Biblical law. But interest as such isn't prohibited.

Before I attempt to prove this from the Old Testament texts, let me point out that in this parable of the talents, Jesus was affirming the importance of productivity and profit. In explaining God's kingdom, He tells the story of a rich man who goes away, but before he goes, he calls three of his stewards and gives them money ("talents"), each according to his abilities (Matthew 25:15). One receives five talents; one receives two talents; and one receives one talent.

The first two doubled their money through trade (25:16, 17). The third one buried his talent in the ground. Upon the rich man's return, each servant came to settle his accounts. The master was most pleased with the first man, who doubled a large

70

amount of capital. He was also pleased with the second, who doubled a smaller amount of capital. To both he said, "Well done, good and faithful servant; you were faithful over a few things, I will make you ruler over many things. Enter into the joy of your lord" (vv. 21, 23).

But to the third man, who buried his talent because of his fear of losing it in trade, the owner was furious. At least the servant could have placed the money with the money changers and received interest back on it.

Jesus was affirming the legitimacy of both profit through trade and the normal rate of return which is secured by lending money. The two forms of activity are not the same, as the parable indicates, but both are legitimate.

Profit through trade is risky. This is why the third man was afraid to attempt it: "And I was afraid, and went and hid your talent in the ground. Look, there you have what is yours" (v. 25). He thought it would be best just to return the owner's principal.

The owner criticized him. Why? Because he had forfeited the use of that talent. The only reason anyone forfeits the use of money is to get a greater amount of money in the future. Otherwise, why not just spend it on whatever it will buy today? Why wait? Thus, *interest* is a basic category of human action. It is inescapable.

Waiting

To show you why interest is inescapable in every aspect of human action, let me give you two examples.

First, assume that I run a national contest. You have just won the grand prize, a brand-new Rolls-Royce automobile. I have paid all the taxes on it. You can either keep it or sell it. It's up to you.

But I come to you and ask you to make a choice. You can take delivery of the car today, or you can take delivery three years from now. Because Rolls-Royce styles don't change very often, and because the car probably won't go down in value, you don't face a loss of capital directly. But you assume that it won't appreciate, either. So what do you do, take delivery now or later?

Obviously, you take delivery of it immediately. Why wait?

What do I have to do to get you to wait? I have to offer you the car, plus something else. Maybe I will toss in a small sedan at the end of three years, or extra money. But to get you to wait for delivery, I have to compensate you, to make it worth your time to wait.

Now, let's take another example. This time, you're the buyer of something from me. You want to buy a piece of property. I show you that you can earn one ounce of gold per year net profit from this land, simply by renting it out. You don't have to do anything. Furthermore, we both agree that the land will probably be able to produce this profit for a thousand years without damage to the land. Then I ask you to pay me one thousand ounces of gold for the land.

You, of course, protest. It isn't worth a thousand ounces. I counter by showing you that you already agreed that the land will produce a thousand ounces of gold, so why shouldn't I be entitled to a thousand ounces? We all agree: equal for equal, right?

Where is my argument incorrect? It has to do with the value to you today of those future ounces of gold. I am asking you to give me gold, ounce for ounce, in advance. But what is the thousandth ounce, a thousand and one years from now, really worth to you? Will you give up an ounce of gold today (and all that it will buy) for that thousandth ounce in the distant future for some unnamed heir of yours? I don't think so.

You apply a discount to that future income. An ounce of gold a thousand years down the road isn't worth as much to you as an ounce is worth to you today. (If it is, please contact me immediately. Do I have a deal for you! There's this bridge in New York City that I know you'll want to buy.) You won't be here to enjoy it.

But think about this principle. An ounce of gold fifty years from now, or twenty years from now, isn't worth an ounce today. It also is discounted in your mind. So is an ounce a year from now. We have therefore discovered a law of human action (which applies in every area of economics): *the present value of future goods is always discounted in comparison with the immediate value of those same goods.*

What is this discount called? I'll bet you've already figured it out. It's called the *rate of interest.*

You discount the future value to you of any good compared to what that same good is worth to you immediately, whether it's that Rolls-Royce or an ounce of gold from that piece of property. For me to get you to hand over the present good today (money), I have to promise to return it to you in the future, plus extra money or other benefit. In other words, I have to pay you *interest.*

In the parable of the talents, the master was angry with the fearful steward because the steward only gave him back his original coin. At the very least, the master said, he could have lent it to the money changers, and have received back some interest.

Banks, Risk, and Interest

Information isn't free of charge. Someone has to pay for it. You may be given it as a gift ("Let me give you a piece of my mind, friend!"), but people seldom value such free advice ("Buddy, I don't think you can spare a piece of *your* mind!"). So usually we have to pay for it. Nobody complains about having to pay for something valuable.

Say that you have a lot of cash. You're a frugal person and concerned about your future. You want to have a "nest egg" for the future. So you're interested in loaning out some of the money.

I come to you and tell you that I know a businessman with a great idea for a profitable investment. He wants a partner to put up the money. He will pay the partner 25% of the profits. But if he goes bankrupt, the partner loses the investment. No, you think to yourself, that's too risky.

You counter with this offer: have the businessman guarantee me out of his own pocket a 10% rate of return on my money, whether the project works or not. Then I'll loan him the money.

What do I do? First, I go to the businessman. He thinks he will be able to make 30% on the money.

Second, I ask myself that magic question: "What's in it for me?" For my trouble in putting the deal together—that is, for my information of where the money is (you) and where the profit opportunity is (the businessman)—I should get something. So I ask the businessman, are you willing to pay 13% for the use of the money? If he says yes, then I come back to you and get the money from you.

The businessman gets his money and the chance at making a lot more. You get your 10% rate of return (your discount of future goods as against present goods), and I get 3% on the deal for my trouble.

That's honest banking. It is the exchange of information. It is also the exchange of risk. You're worried about your *risks in the future*. You want more money to deal with those risks. The businessman worries about the risks of guaranteeing the creditor (me) 13%, but he feels that the risk is worth it. I worry about the risks of the businessman going bankrupt and fleeing the country, since I have to pay you your 10%. But I figure it's worth my risk.

We have *voluntarily exchanged risk*. Each person is now more comfortable with his own fears. Each man gets something for his trouble. We all bear risk, but we bear an amount of risk that's closer to what we want than would have been possible if I, the deal-putter-together, had not come onto the scene.

As you have probably recognized, I am the banker in this example.

A bank is not an evil institution. It is a marvelous institution in principle. It allows the profitable exchange of information and the profitable exchange of risk. Those who participate all believe that they will be better off with this institution than without it.

The fact is, banking has been one of the crucial institutions in the development of the modern world. It fulfills valid economic desires. It allows us all to deal more successfully with an uncertain (completely unknown) and risky (partially unknown) future. Banking allows us to *spread our risks*.

The Marks of Honest Banking

There must be a lender. We call him the *depositor*. He has to give up the use of his money for a specified period of time. In exchange, he is offered a specified rate of interest, to be paid to him in addition to the return of his original invested money when the loan comes due.

There must be a *borrower*. He is someone who believes that his opportunities for putting the capital to use outweighs the expense (and risk) of having to repay the principal plus the interest. He may be a producer. He may be a consumer. But he brings collateral to the table (his past performance, his future prospects, his idea, etc.) and promises to repay.

There must be an *evaluator*. This is the banker. He assesses the risk of not being repaid. He bears the risk of paying off the depositor if the borrower defaults. He must evaluate the credit worthiness of the borrower. He gets paid for his trouble by the *spread*: the difference between the rate of interest the borrower pays him and the rate of interest he pays the depositor *after the transaction is over*.

There is nothing immoral about such transactions. The Bible nowhere prohibits them, with one exception: charity loans. (I shall cover these later on.) These sorts of transactions are expected to be beneficial to all the participants, *or else the participants wouldn't enter into such transactions voluntarily*.

In the next chapter, I will discuss some highly immoral aspects of a perverted form of banking. But as I have outlined banking here, there is nothing wrong with it. The key to bear in mind is the question of *the use of the money*. The depositor *gives up* the use of his money during the period of the loan. He can't get something for nothing. If he gets a rate of interest, he gets it because he doesn't have the use of his money in the interim. When he loans it out, *it is no longer his money*. He has given up ownership and use of *present money* in exchange for *future money*. He doesn't get something (a rate of interest) for nothing (no true transfer of ownership). Whenever this fundamental transfer of ownership is violated, banking becomes immoral, as I shall show in the next chapter.

What if the depositor needs "his" money back early? That shouldn't be too hard. He goes to the banker and makes a loan request. The banker knows that the businessman is probably going to repay the loan. The banker can make a loan to the depositor out of bank capital, or he can loan him money from another depositor's account, with the note from the original businessman as collateral.

But to get money now, the depositor either takes a discount (doesn't get all the money originally agreed to be repaid), or else he has to promise to repay the bank extra money when the repayment of the loan falls due. The point is, nobody gets something for nothing. The depositor is asking for money that has been loaned out. It isn't in the bank any longer. To get "his" money early, he has to borrow it from someone else, for during the period of the loan, *it isn't his money any more*.

All this is fairly easy to understand. There are no hidden secrets here. Banking fundamentals aren't mysterious. It's simply a method of exchanging present and future risks, present and future goods, with a middleman who puts the deals together. And it's all governed by this rule: "You don't get something for nothing."

Charity Loans

The Old Testament forbade lenders from making interest-bearing loans to *poverty-stricken brothers in the faith*. "If you lend money to any of My people *who are poor* among you, you shall not be like a moneylender [usurer—KJV]; you shall not charge him interest [usury—KJV]" (Exodus 22:25, emphasis added). The New American Standard Version reads: "If you lend money to My people, to the poor among you, you are not to act as a creditor to him; you shall not charge him interest."

The Bible is not speaking here simply about money loans. Interest is a phenomenon that relates to all human action, so this prohibition applies on any sort of loan. "And if one of your brethren becomes poor, and falls into poverty among you, then you shall help him. . . . Take no usury or interest from him; but fear your God, that your brother may live with you. You shall not lend him your money for usury, nor lend him your food at a profit" (Leviticus 25:35a, 36-37). Notice: it speaks of the *poor* brother. This is not a prohibition against business loans.

The warning against profiting from charitable loans from those who share the faith is clear: "One who increases his possessions by usury and extortion gathers it for him who will pity the poor" (Proverbs 28:8). In other words, the evil man lays up treasure unjustly, but the righteous man will eventually earn it back. This is in line with another promise of Proverbs, "the wealth of the sinner is stored up for the righteous" (13:22b).

Yes, the lender who lends money to a poor fellow believer can legitimately ask only for a return of the principal. He must not ask for anything extra. This means that he forfeits the interest that might otherwise have been earned in some sort of business loan. The lender suffers a loss, for he forfeits the use of his capital over time, and bears the risk that the loan will never be repaid. But God will reward the generous lender, Proverbs says. In effect, God pays the interest payment to the righteous lender. God becomes a kind of heavenly co-signer of the poor man's note. Specifically, the generous lender will prosper at the expense of the unrighteous exploiter in a society which is governed by the law of God.

Summary

Lending money at interest isn't immoral and shouldn't be made illegal. It shouldn't be controlled by the State in any way. The Bible teaches that loans at interest to poor fellow believers should not be made, but the Bible is equally emphatic that it is God who punishes this type of loan. There is no mention of any civil penalties. It is a religious matter. Someone has to define "fellow believer" and "poor." This is not something the civil authorities should concern themselves with. At most, church authorities might penalize usurers, not the State.

But most loans in a society are business loans or loans made to people who have credit references and collateral. These are not poor people. They come with *credit worthiness*. This is a true *capital asset.* A man's reputation as an honest and efficient businessman who pays his debts (and has few of them) is certainly a valuable asset. It can be borrowed against under certain circumstances. Certainly, by putting collateral against the loan, he adds to his credibility.

Why should someone with a great idea to serve consumers but without enough cash on hand to finance the initial delivery of this service or product not be allowed to seek out other people to put up the money? Why shouldn't others be allowed to share this vision and share in the rewards? Some people may want an "equity" position: shares of ownership in the business, rain or shine, boom or bust. Others may not want to become entrepreneurs, but they are willing to forgo the use of their money for an interest return. Jesus teaches in His parable of the talents that both kinds of investments are legitimate: higher-risk profit seeking, as well as guaranteed-return interest seeking.

The fundamentals of Biblical banking are these:

1. The King James translators erroneously translated the Greek word for "interest" as "usury."
2. Usury in the Old Testament refers exclusively to interest taken from a poor fellow-believer.
3. Jesus described the kingdom of God in terms of profit seeking and interest seeking: a positive rate of return.
4. Interest is a basic category of human action; it is inescapable.
5. It arises from the fact that we discount the present value of future goods as against what those same goods are worth to us right now.
6. Information isn't a free good; someone pays for it.
7. Some people prefer to lend money at a high enough rate of interest, as a means of providing for themselves in the future.
8. Other people have needs and opportunities that they prefer to satisfy now, and pay for through interest owed in the future.
9. Middlemen bring these two sorts of people together; these middlemen are called bankers.
10. Their information isn't free.
11. They make their money through the "spread": the difference

between interest promised to them by the borrower and interest promised by them to the depositor.

12. Through lending and borrowing, people exchange degrees of risk.

13. The key to honest banking is the transfer of ownership of the capital asset: what is lent to the borrower cannot simultaneously be used by the lender.

14. Charity loans to poor fellow believers should not have any interest payment attached to them.

15. God rewards the generous, zero-interest lender to the poor.

8

FRACTIONAL RESERVE BANKING

If you ever take your neighbor's garment as a pledge, you shall return it to him before the sun goes down. For that is his only covering, it is his garment for his skin. What will he sleep in? And it will be that when he cries to Me, I will hear, for I am gracious (Exodus 22:26-27).

The context of this verse is the general prohibition of interest taken from a poor fellow believer. He has been reduced to such abject poverty that he asks the neighbor for a loan so small that his coat can serve as collateral. He has nothing else of value that can serve as collateral. This is not a business loan.

But think about the purpose of collateral. If I give you a loan, I want some security that I will get something from you if you refuse to repay it or are unable to repay it. Perhaps I loan you money against an automobile you own. If you default on the loan, I can repossess the automobile and sell it. Maybe I can get my money back this way.

Also, I know that you don't want to lose that automobile. You will work hard to earn enough money to repay me. I know that the pain you will experience by losing your collateral spurs you on to greater efforts. I don't have to take physical possession of the property, if I have taken possession of legal title which entitles me to take physical possession, should you default on the loan.

But what about a poor man who has no collateral besides his cloak? I want to get him to pay off the loan. Still, the cloak is useless to me personally. I would want to use it at night, when it gets cold, but I can't. I have to return it to him every evening. So it is useless to me. Or is it?

Obviously, it is useful to him. He gets cold at night, so he comes to get it. It is a lot of trouble for him (and a bit humiliating) to have to come to my place every evening to get back his cloak. He wants to get out of debt as soon as possible. So it does serve as an incentive for him to repay, which also means that it is an asset to me.

There is another aspect of this sort of collateral which most people never think of. What if the borrower is corrupt in his heart? What if he went out and borrowed money from a dozen people, with the cloak as collateral? He promised each lender: "Look, if I default, you may have my cloak. I want my cloak, so I surely won't default." But if he has borrowed against the cloak twelve times over, he may be perfectly willing to default on that cloak. Let the lenders decide who gets the collateral.

The corrupt debtor shouts, "Tough luck, suckers. Sort it out among yourselves. The money is gone. All I have left is the cloak. I'll be cold without it, but I had fun with the money. It was worth it!"

What the Bible teaches is that it is immoral to secure multiple loans with the same piece of collateral. To reduce the possibility of someone indebting himself several times over, the Bible allows the lender to take physical possession of the collateral daily. Since only one lender can do this per day, the debtor is not able to indebt himself many times over on the basis of one piece of collateral.

Just because a piece of collateral is *physically useless* to the lender does not mean that it is *economically useless* to him. It may be very useful to him economically, first, to motivate the debtor to repay the loan, and second, to prohibit the borrower from indebting himself several times over.

Multiple Indebtedness

In Chapter Three I discussed the creation of a warehouse receipt for storing gold or silver. A person brings in ten ounces of gold to the warehouse for safekeeping, and the warehouse issues a receipt for ten ounces of gold. The owner pays a fee for storing the money, but he presumably increases the safety of his holdings. The warehouse specializes in protecting money metals from burglars. The depositor pays for this specialized service. It is somewhat like a safety deposit box in a bank, except that the warehouse issues a receipt.

The receipt may begin to function as money. If people trust the warehouse, they will accept a receipt for all or part of this gold in payment for goods and services. Why not? A piece of paper authorizing the bearer to collect a specified amount of gold is just about the same as the actual ounce of gold. Besides, the gold is safer in storage, and paper is a lot more convenient than pieces of metal.

But a problem threatens the system. What if the warehouse owner recognizes that people in the community trust him? They know that he has a lot of guards watching everything, and that he has always been scrupulously honest. He then betrays this trust. He issues warehouse receipts for gold for which there is no gold in reserve.

He then loans these receipts to borrowers. The receipts serve as money. People accept them in exchange for goods and services. These warehouse receipts are considered "as good as gold." Why not? They are always exchangeable for gold upon demand. Just take the piece of paper to the warehouse, and get your gold. No problem!

But now there *is* a problem. There are more receipts for gold than gold in reserve to pay all the potential bearers on demand. These "demand deposits" are now vulnerable to that most feared of financial events, a *bank run*. Depositors who have receipts come down and demand repayment. But there isn't enough gold in reserve to meet the total demand.

The warehouse has placed itself in a similar position as the poor man who immorally secures loans from a dozen lenders on the basis of one piece of collateral. The warehouse owner has become a banker. He makes loans, for which borrowers agree to pay him interest in the future, along with a return of the principal. But the money, once loaned out, is gone until the day that repayment comes. The warehouse is vulnerable to a run on the deposits. The warehouse owes gold to the depositors. It is indebted to them. The deposits are legal liabilities to the bank. The bank has become indebted many times over. It has in reserve only a fraction of the assets promised to depositors.

There is a name used by economists to describe such banking practices: *fractional reserve banking*. Banks do not have 100% of all their liabilities on hand as assets against those liabilities. In short, their reserves are only a *fraction* of their liabilities (deposits). They have loaned out the money long term, but their clients (depositors, lenders to them) can demand their money short term. Thus, the *time factor* intervenes. This is the weak point of all modern banking.

The Creation of Money

Remember, I said that the warehouse receipt circulated as if it were gold. Therefore, if gold serves as money in that society, the pieces of paper will also serve as money.

When these pieces of paper are pure money-metal substitutes, nothing changes. Physical gold is taken out of circulation and put into a warehouse. A piece of paper (a warehouse receipt) substitutes for the physical gold. No new money has come into circulation. No money has been taken out of circulation. Nothing fundamental changes, except for convenience.

But if the warehouse owner writes up a warehouse receipt for gold when there is no new gold on deposit, then he has increased the money supply in the community. No one has come to the warehouse and deposited gold (taken it out of the day-to-day economy). So the warehouse receipt is inescapably *inflationary*. It is an addition of money into the economy. (I am defining "inflation" as "an increase in the money supply," the way dictionaries and economists defined it 50 years ago. The result is rising prices, or else prices will not fall as far as they would otherwise have fallen.)

Here is what normally would happen. The warehouse receipt circulates as if it were gold. If the warehouse owner is very cautious, and issues only a few extra receipts, probably nobody will find out. He will collect a little interest from borrowers, and everyone will be happy. Prices may rise only a little, or perhaps not at all.

But other warehouse owners hear about their competitor. So he's lending out money, is he? Well, two can play that game. So they begin to issue their warehouse receipts to borrowers. They too get in on the banking game. The money supply now starts to increase.

Prices start to rise as denominated in gold. But gold's price doesn't rise initially, for all the receipts are "as good as gold" and therefore identical to gold, supposedly. So those who hold gold get hurt. They see the price of other goods rising, but stodgy old gold stays the same. So they do the rational thing: they start buying goods before the price of these goods gets any higher. They go down to the store and start buying goods with warehouse receipts. All of a sudden, the store owners see a lot of paper receipts. Where did all these receipts come from? Something funny is going on. Maybe banks are issuing phony receipts. Maybe it would be smart to cash in these receipts and demand delivery of gold.

They go to the warehouses and start demanding gold. All of a sudden, the run on the warehouse begins. The warehouse receipts begin to fall in value compared to gold. Other people rush down to get their gold (which is now rising in value compared to the warehouse receipts they are holding). The bank collapses. Or else it is forced to delay repayment to receipt owners.

It is similar to the wicked cloak owner who has indebted himself many times over, and then leaves his creditors standing out in the cold.

The Shrinking of Money

A few days before the bank run, business had been booming. Everyone seemed to have lots of money to spend. It was terrific for businessmen.

A few days after the bank run, reality sets in. Many depositors can't get their money. People who have borrowed from the banks because business was so great discover that their investments have gone sour. They had begun building new factories, but now there is no more demand for the goods produced by these factories. They had been lured into making the investment (borrowing the money) because the economy seemed to be booming, and interest rates were nice and low.

The reason interest rates were so low is that the banks were counterfeiting money and lending it out. They didn't have to pay depositors any interest, and they were taking in interest. It was so easy.

The day of economic judgment arrives. Businesses go bankrupt. Others lay off employees. Everyone has to adjust to the new conditions of supply and demand. The inflation is over; deflation has come. Some bank notes (warehouse receipts) are worthless. They aren't money any more. People who held them have lost their money. They stop spending as much as before.

Does this sound familiar? It should. It's called a depression. And there is one cause, and *only one cause*, of depressions: *prior inflations*. The good days looked so good; the bad days look so bad. People were lied to. The counterfeit warehouse receipts were promissory notes, and these promises were lies. The reality of the post-lying era is like a hangover after a night of reveling. But it *is* reality. The drunk, like the businessman, should be thankful for it. They seldom are.

Look, depressions are hard to explain. Why should virtually every businessman in the country—even in the world (1930's)—all make the same mistakes at about the same time. Sure, businessmen make mistakes. Some buy when they ought to be selling. Some win, and others lose. But not in a depression. Why do almost all of them make the same mistake at about the same time?

The answer is the money system. All businessmen are tied to money and interest rates. If we want to explain why almost all of them think a boom is going to continue when a bust is about to occur, we need to look at money and interest rates. The businessmen make the same mistakes because *interest rates are giving them incorrect signals*.

Borrowing rates are low because bankers are creating counterfeit money—*legal* counterfeit money—and loaning it out. Then inflation hits, the economy booms, and then craters when the bankers slow down the printing of money in self-defense against bank runs: too many receipts for too few reserves. Money shrinks (or even just slows down), and the depression hits.

We've seen it before: the boom of 1964-69 turned into the bust of 1969-71. The boom of 1972-74 turned into the bust of 1975-76. The boom of 1977-79 turned into the bust of 1980-82. It will happen again. It always does.

That's the curse of counterfeit money.

Pure Counterfeit Money

The modern banking system has gone a long way in the last fifty years. All over the world, nations abandoned the gold standard. The citizens are no longer given legal access to true warehouse receipts (gold-backed money). They can't take their paper receipts to a bank or the national treasury and demand a fixed, predictable quantity of gold (or silver) on demand.

Now the bankers don't have to worry about a "bank run" against gold. Neither do the politicians. The result has been mass inflation all over the world. You could buy a three-bedroom home in 1913 for under $3,000.

Today, the game is played differently. Let's see how it works. Say that you take in $100 cash and deposit it in your bank. The central bank (in the United States, the Federal Reserve System) requires banks to keep varying percentages of money on reserve at the Fed itself, in non-interest-paying accounts. A 10% reserve makes it easy to compute, though for many accounts it's under 5%.

The bank takes your $100 and issues you a receipt (bank deposit slip) for $100. It then takes $10 and wires it to the regional Federal Reserve bank. Then it loans out the remaining $90.

The guy who borrows the $90 deposits it into his account. Presumably, he then writes a check for the $90. The person who gets his check deposits it. His banker takes 10%, or $9, and wires it to the regional Federal Reserve Bank. Then he loans out the remaining $81. The borrower writes a check to someone who deposits it in his bank. His banker takes 10%, or $8.10, wires it to the Federal Reserve Bank, and loans out $72.90.

And so it goes, from bank to bank, merrily multiplying. In theory, that original $100 cash deposit (or check) creates an additional $800 in loaned money, plus your original $100.

And you wonder why we have inflation?

You think I'm making this up? Then take a look at the official explanation of how the system works. It was published by the Federal Reserve System itself in 1963, on the 50th anniversary of the creation of the Fed (in 1913), a book called *The Federal Reserve System: Purposes and Functions*. The numbers are different because the example uses a more conservative 20% reserve requirement instead of today's 10% (or lower). But you can see how it works, according to the people who run this country's banking and monetary system. With a 20% reserve requirement, a $100 deposit multiplies by 5: the original $100 plus $400 in "phantom" money — which is *real, legal money.*

MULTIPLYING CAPACITY OF RESERVE MONEY
THROUGH BANK TRANSACTIONS[1]
(in dollars)

Transactions	Deposited in checking accounts	Lent	Set aside as reserves
Bank 1	100.00	80.00	20.00
2	80.00	64.00	16.00
3	64.00	51.20	12.80
4	51.20	40.96	10.24
5	40.96	32.77	8.19
6	32.77	26.22	6.55
7	26.22	20.98	5.24
8	20.98	16.78	4.20
9	16.78	13.42	3.36
10	13.42	10.74	2.68
Total for 10 banks	446.33	357.07	89.26
Additional banks............	53.67	[2]42.93	[2]10.74
Grand total, all banks......	500.00	400.00	100.00

[1]Assuming an average member bank reserve requirement of 20 per cent of demand deposits.
[2]Adjusted to offset rounding in previous figures.

Problem: If Mexico defaults on its $100 million in loans, or Brazil defaults on its $110 million, what then? What kind of run on the banks will we see then? And if the Federal Reserve System inflates money to cover these losses, can you imagine what the multiplication effects will be?

Isn't legalized counterfeiting wonderful? Something for nothing. We'll all be rich soon. Millionaires. But bread will cost $40 a loaf.

Then we'll have a depression. The politicians will blame businessmen. The bankers will blame anyone. Everyone will blame capitalism. But capitalism wasn't the cause of the boom or the collapse; fractional reserve banking was: too many warehouse receipts with too little money in reserve.

Summary

Banking as a purely lender and borrower operation is a wonderful institution. Pure banking is not inflationary. If I loan you $100, I can't use that $100 while you're using it. I don't have a "demand deposit." I can't demand the money I loaned you until the date that repayment is due.

Then you deposit the $100 temporarily in a demand deposit account. But your banker can't loan it out or pay you interest. Then you spend it. The same $100 goes through the economy *without multiplying*.

Not so in a fractional reserve banking system. I have the right at any time to spend the money I deposited, even though 90% of it (or more) was loaned out already. Where does the banker get the money to honor my check? From some depositor who deposited his paycheck today.

It's just like the fellow who owns that warehouse. He issues lots of extra warehouse receipts for money (gold) because he knows that very few depositors will come down on any day and demand their gold. If someone does, probably this will be offset by some other depositor who is depositing gold in the warehouse. It all looks so easy, until the run occurs.

Fractional reserve banking violates the Biblical principle

against multiple indebtedness. When bankers violate this law (with the consent of the State), it leads to inflation and economic booms, followed by deflation and economic depressions. Fractional reserve banking is a form of fraud, as surely as a borrower who uses one piece of collateral to get a dozen loans is fraudulent. But at least "cloak banking" isn't inflationary. The money that lenders loan to the fraudulent cloak owner goes from them to him, but it doesn't multiply. He wins; they lose. The businessmen who sell to him win; the businessmen who would otherwise have sold to them lose.

Fractional reserve banking is inflationary. A single piece of collateral (deposit) is used by the banking system as a whole to create multiple liabilities against the banks as a system.

Here is how the system produces evil:

1. Using a single piece of collateral to borrow money and therefore to create multiple indebtedness is prohibited by the Bible.

2. A lawful warehouse receipt must have whatever is promised on reserve for immediate delivery.

3. A warehouse receipt to any item which serves the community as money must also be fully backed with the weight and fineness promised on the receipt.

4. The issuing of unbacked warehouse receipts to a money commodity is a form of counterfeiting.

5. Counterfeiting is an addition of new money into the economy.

6. The addition of new money into an economy is inflationary.

7. The new money creates an illusion of prosperity: economic boom.

8. The boom leads to further borrowing by businessmen.

9. Interest rates stay low *temporarily* because counterfeiters are creating new money to loan.

10. Prices rise.

11. People get suspicious of the warehouse receipts.

12. A run on the warehouse occurs.

13. The public loses confidence in the warehouse receipts and the boom.

14. The money supply shrinks.

15. The boom turns into a bust: deflationary depression.

16. The depression brings everyone to economic reality.

17. People hate painful reality.

18. The government is tempted to create new money, or have the banks do it for them, to stimulate a new boom.

19. Capitalism doesn't cause depressions; fraudulent banking and government inflation cause booms, then depressions.

9

PROTECTING LICENSED COUNTERFEITERS

You shall do no injustice in judgment. You shall not be partial to the poor, nor honor the person of the mighty. But in righteousness you shall judge your neighbor (Leviticus 19:15).

Three counterfeiters are discovered. The first one is a middle-class man who owns a cheap offset printing press. He has printed 500 $20 bills and spent them into circulation.

The second one is a U.S. government official. He works for the Bureau of Engraving and Printing. He has printed up a million $20 bills, and the government has spent them into circulation.

The third is the Chairman of the Board of a multi-billion-dollar New York bank. His bank has loaned a billion dollars of fractionally reserve bank money to Mexico's government-owned petroleum company, Pemex. The price of oil has collapsed, so Pemex can't pay its bills.

What happens to the three counterfeiters? The first man is convicted of counterfeiting and is sent to jail. The second man works until age 65 and is given a pension.

But what about the third man, the chairman? Here is where it could get interesting. The third man goes to the nation's central bank, the Federal Reserve System, which in turn calls the Mexican government, which immediately prints a Mexican bond for $25 million, which is then bought by the Federal Reserve System with electronic money created out of nothing. This Mexican bond then becomes part of the "legal reserve" which supposedly undergirds the U.S. monetary system. (This was made legal in the infamous Monetary Control Act of 1980, against which only 13 congressmen voted.)

The Mexican government sends the money to Pemex, which then remits $25 million to pay this quarter's interest payment to the New York bank. Pemex pays the bank a fee for "rolling over" the loan. Three months from now, another $25 million will fall due. The chairman of the New York bank gets a round of applause from the bank's board of directors, and perhaps even a bonus for his brilliant delaying of the bank's crisis for another three months.

The $25 million then multiplies through the U.S. fractional reserve banking system, creating millions of new commercial dollars in a mini-wave of inflation.

This scenario could really take place, given United States law. Is this system just? Would you say that the law respects neither the mighty nor the poor man?

The Federal Reserve System

In late November of 1910 (probably November 22), a private coach carrying some of the nation's leading bankers and a U.S. Senator pulled out of the Hoboken, New Jersey, train station and headed for Georgia. Their ultimate destination: Jekyll Island, which was owned by some of the richest men on earth as a hunting club. Membership in the club was by inheritance only.

On board that train was Senator Nelson Aldrich, the maternal grandfather of Nelson Aldrich Rockefeller. Also aboard: Henry P. Davison, a senior partner in the powerful banking firm of J. P. Morgan Co., Benjamin Strong (another Morgan employee), and a European expert in banking, Paul Warburg. Representatives of two other major New York banking firms were also present.

The reporters who gathered at the train station were told nothing, except that the men were all going duck shooting. Six years later, Bertie Forbes, the man who founded *Forbes* magazine, reported briefly on the meeting, and most people thought the whole story was just a "yarn." Very little has been written on it since 1916. (Probably the most detailed account is chapter 24 of the highly favorable biography, *Nelson W. Aldrich*, by Nathaniel W. Stephenson [Scribner's Sons, 1930; reprinted by Kennikat Press, 1971.])

At that secret meeting, these men designed what became the

Federal Reserve System, the central bank of the United States.

As they were returning, they were met by reporters at the Brunswick, Georgia train station. Davison went to meet with them, and when he returned, he informed the group that "they won't give us away." They never did. The press never mentioned the meeting.

Senator Aldrich, a Republican, was the political middleman. His biographer Stephenson reveals this information:

> How was the Reserve Bank to be controlled? The experience of the two United States Banks, in our early history, pointed a warning. The experience of a life time spoke in Aldrich's unconditional reply. It was to be kept out of politics. It must not be controlled by Congress. The government was to be represented in the board of directors, it was to have full knowledge of all the Bank's affairs but a majority of the directors were to be chosen, directly or indirectly, by the members of the association (p. 379).

Republican Aldrich did not succeed in getting his version of the central bank through Congress in 1911 and 1912, but Democratic President Woodrow Wilson got a very similar version passed in December of 1913. Thus, in the year of the income tax was also born the Federal Reserve System, our nation's central bank.

A Big Bank Insurance Company

The Federal Reserve Bank is the most powerful insurance company in the United States, and perhaps in the world. Its function is to control the money supply of the U.S., inflating or (hardly ever) deflating at will the total money supply. It was created, the founders promised, in order to eliminate "panics," as recessions and depressions were called in those days. The result:

> The "panic" of 1920-21
> The depression of 1929-39
> The recession of 1953-54
> The recession of 1957-58
> The recession of 1969-70
> The recession of 1975-76
> The recession of 1980-82

It was created, we were told, in order to supply a so-called "elastic currency" to meet the seasonal needs of business. This "elastic currency" has stretched into the hundreds of billions, ever upward.

What it was *really* created for was to prevent the bankruptcy of any major commercial New York bank, and other major banks around the country. Only one major bank in the United States failed in the Great Depression, the private commercial bank with the official-sounding name, the Bank of the United States. But over 9,000 small banks suspended payments.

Even in the case of the Bank of the United States, we can see the hand of the big banks. This bank was financed primarily by small merchants, especially Jewish merchants. It was not an "insider's" bank. The Clearing House banks, made up of the major New York banks, at first promised to allow the faltering bank to merge with more solvent institutions, but at the last moment they pulled out of the bail-out, allowing the besieged bank to suffer more runs by depositors. This created a wave of runs on other banks. Finally, in December of 1930, the State of New York shut it down to prevent total bankruptcy. It eventually paid off over 83% of its liabilities after it liquidated its assets. The question can at least be raised concerning the reasons for the Clearing House banks' refusal to help it in the moment of crisis. Was it their fear of its total collapse? Or were they simply eliminating a "non-traditional," more speculative rival that had profited from the boom of 1924-29?

This rival eliminated, there were no more big-bank failures for the remainder of the depression.

In any case, this bankruptcy indicates the Achilles' heel of fractional reserve banking: the money was "invested long" in long-term mortgages, but the bank's liabilities were short-term: cash on demand. But the cash was gone. Such is the reality of issuing more receipts for short-term money than there is short-term money in reserve.

The Fed was also created to supply funds to keep a bank panic from spreading to the major banks. The key phrase is "supply funds"—a synonym of *inflate*.

The Federal Reserve Bank is a privately owned corporation whose shares of ownership are held by the member banks. It is quasi-public, in that the President of the United States appoints the members of the Board of Governors of the Fed, but the directors of the 12 regional Fed banks, and especially the powerful New York Federal Reserve Bank, are not appointed by any political body. There are nine directors of each regional Federal Reserve Bank; six are appointed by local bankers, and three by the Board of Governors of the Federal Reserve System.

Can the government tell the Fed what to do? If Congress and the President are agreed about what to do, yes. If there is disagreement over monetary policy—and there usually is—then the Fed does pretty much what it wants. What the origin of the Fed indicates is that the Fed does what the major multinational banks want. What the House and Senate committees on bank regulation want is usually unclear, and a majority of the members barely know what a central bank is, let alone how it functions or—wonder of wonders—who actually *owns* it. They don't even ask. It's considered "bad form," a breach of etiquette. I know from experience. I served as a research assistant for a Congressman who was a member of the House Banking Committee.

The Monetization of Debt

This is an invention of the modern world. A government needs money. It fears a tax revolt if it raises taxes. It cannot afford to pay more interest, so it can't borrow money from the general public. It therefore goes to the central bank and says, "Buy our Treasury debt certificates."

The Treasury creates the debt certificates (usually on a computer entry: liability). The central bank buys them by creating another entry: money. The computer blips are swapped.

The government has just *monetized* some of its debt. It pays a lower rate of interest *initially* to the central bank than it would have to pay if it went into the free market to *compete* for borrowed money.

What's wrong with this? Who gets hurt? Holders of money

will be hurt. The central bank creates a reserve asset when it buys the government bond. The money is then used by the government to buy whatever it wants (mainly votes). This new money goes through the economy. If the banking system is a fractional reserve system, the money multiplies many times over. This is the process of legalized counterfeiting we call inflation.

The government never gets something for nothing. That means that you and I aren't going to get something for nothing. More likely, we'll get nothing for something. We will get higher prices, higher long-term interest rates, and then a recession. We will go through the boom-bust cycle that the inflated money creates.

The monetization of debt is the easy way out for the government, meaning the easy way to confiscate our capital.

The best solution: no more government debt. Owe no man anything, including as a taxpayer.

When the Fed purchases any asset (most of its assets consist of U.S. 90-day Treasury bills), it creates the money. But it buys the bonds from a favored group of about 20 major banks and securities trading houses that deal in U.S. securities, and which in turn collect commissions on each transaction. (The process is described in a booklet sent free of charge by the New York Federal Reserve Bank, *Open Market Operations*. Order from 33 Liberty Street, New York, NY 10045.)

On November 21, 1985, one day short of 75 years after that train pulled out of the Hoboken station, the Bank of New York, a private commercial bank, experienced a computer failure. That day it had purchased $22.6 billion in U.S. government securities from other banks and securities dealers, to be transferred to the Federal Reserve. The sales orders came in, but the bank couldn't get the money back out when its computer system "crashed." The Fed had to loan that bank $22.6 billion over the weekend to cover the payments it owed to the other banks and dealers. The Fed paid off the other banks directly. (The bank did have to pay the Fed interest for the weekend use of the money, which amounted to several million dollars. Some computer error!)

Do you think your local bank could get a tide-me-over loan of $22.6 billion?

Question: Why doesn't the Fed buy these bonds directly? Answer: because it wouldn't generate commissions for the favored 20 banks.

The government allows the central bank, legally a private organization, to manipulate the money supply of the United States. The central banks of every nation possess this same prerogative. Why do the governments tolerate it? Because they always need money. The central banks stand as "lenders of last resort" to the government.

The government pays interest on the Treasury bills held by the Federal Reserve. It amounts to about $15 billion a year these days. At the end of the year, the Fed sends back about 85% of this money to the U.S. Treasury. It keeps 15% for "handling." (It pays for all check-clearing transactions in the U.S., for example.)

The Fed's Declaration of Independence

The Fed has never been audited by any agency of the United States government. The Fed's officials have resisted every effort of any congressman or senator to impose an audit by the Government Accounting Office (GAO).

The Federal Reserve Board meets to formulate U.S. economic policy every few months. No information on the Board's decisions can be released to anyone, including the President of the United States, for 45 days. The Fed says so, and Congress won't call the Fed's bluff. It used to be 90 days, but Congress forced the Fed to speed up the reporting date. Fed chairman Paul Volcker protested strongly. He said such a release of information interferes with the decision-making ability of the Fed.

The U.S. money supply is totally regulated by decisions of the Board of Governors of the Federal Reserve System. The Fed establishes the "reserve requirements" of the commercial banks (10%, 5%, or whatever, depending on where the bank is located, and whether it's a checking account or a savings account). The Fed buys or sells U.S. Treasury bills (U.S. government debt certificates). When the Fed buys, it increases the money supply (multiplying because of fractional reserves). When it sells, it deflates the money supply (shrinking by this same multiplication number).

But it never sells for more than a few weeks. It is almost always buying. It is almost always inflating.

Thus, the American business cycle ("boom and bust") is controlled by a handful of men who are not directly controlled by the President or the Congress, except in those rare instances when the Legislature and the Executive agree completely and press their decision on the Fed.

Oh yes, I forgot to mention that *the Fed owns the entire U.S. gold stock.* Legally, there is no "United States" gold stock. There is only the Fed's gold stock. It is stored, not in Fort Knox, Kentucky, but at 33 Liberty Street, New York City, New York. The U.S. government has always sold its gold to the Fed, beginning in 1914.

Where did the Fed get the money to buy the gold? It created it, of course. In short, it *counterfeited* it. But it's legal.

What is really choice is that in 1933, the U.S. government outlawed the private ownership of gold. It bought all the gold it could forcibly collect from the public, paying the going price of $20.67 per ounce. Then it sold it to the Fed at $20.67 per ounce. The next year, the government raised the price of gold to $35 an ounce. Net profit to the Fed: 75%.

This raised the legal reserves for banks, and the money supply (so-called M-1) zipped upward by 30%, 1933 to 1935.

"No!" you say to yourself. "It couldn't be true. The government confiscated our gold in 1933 so that a private corporation owned by the member banks could buy it at a discount? Impossible!"

All right, my skeptical friend, pick up a copy of any Friday edition of *The Wall Street Journal*. Somewhere in the second section (they always shift it around) you will find a table called **Federal Reserve Data**. Check the listing under "Member Bank Reserve Changes." You will see a quotation for "Gold Stock." It never changes: $11,090,000,000. They don't sell it, and it's kept on the books at the meaningless arbitrary price of $42.22 per ounce.

Whose reserves? *Member banks*. Who holds title? *The Federal Reserve System*. Who owns the Federal Reserve? *Member banks*.

This leads me to conclude that if you're going to become a counterfeiter, you might as well become an audacious one. The backyard operators risk going to jail. Central bankers don't.

Sure, by law, Congress and the President could demand that the Fed sell the gold back at $42.22 per ounce. By law. Have you ever seen anyone propose such a law? Has Congress ever brought it up for consideration since 1913? Have you seen anyone discuss the wisdom, or even the possibility, of such a law, except for "kooks" who write newsletters and paperback books? Have you ever heard of a Ph.D.-holding university economist recommending it? No? Neither have I.

Sure, Congress controls the Fed. Legally, the Fed must report to Congress. Just as the Politburo in the Soviet Union must report to the Russian people.

Congress can get its gold back any time it wants to. Just as an alcoholic can quit drinking any time he wants to. Just as American private citizens can get *their* gold back from Congress at $42.22 per ounce (or even at a market price), any time we want to.

If you believe this, I've still got that New York bridge to sell you.

The Depositors' Insurance

The Federal Deposit Insurance Corporation came into existence in 1934, the year after the government confiscated the public's gold. The FDIC is promoted as a government-guaranteed insurance program for private citizens' bank accounts. Well, as they say, yes and no.

No, it isn't an agency of the Federal government. No, the government has never promised to bail it out if it gets swamped with banks that are going bankrupt. No, the Joint Resolution of Congress in 1980 to insure every bank account up to $100,000 isn't a law. The President never signed it, so it isn't a law. There has never been any such law.

Yes, if the FDIC really did look as though it was about to go bankrupt, either the Fed or Congress would almost certainly act to bail it out. The Fed would print the money, just as it did when the Continental Illinois Bank almost went under in 1983, and it had to pump about $4.5 billion into it. The bankers don't want a bank run.

Could the FDIC bail out the banks in a panic? Of course not. It has about $1 on reserve for every $100 in deposits. This "reserve" is in fact nothing except U.S. Treasury bills: government bonds, in other words. To get the cash, the FDIC has to cash in these bonds and get the U.S. Treasury to pay cash. Two bankruptcies the size of Continental Illinois would deplete the FDIC's reserves to zero, or close to it.

The FDIC is an illusion whose purpose is to calm down depositors who might otherwise make runs on weak banks and crash the economy into a depression. The FDIC was created to *reduce risks for bankers*, so that at least the biggest banks don't face such crises. Then the bankers can go out and loan hundreds of millions of the depositors' dollars to "Third World" nations that never intend to pay back any of the money.

In a gold-standard country—none exists any more—the people can put the pressure on banks and the government to stop inflating the currency, simply by going down to the bank or the Treasury and buying gold at the fixed, government-defined price. Pretty soon the government has to stop inflating. Pretty soon, a bank which has issued too many phony warehouse receipts gets threatened by a panic run.

Then one of two things happens:

1. The bank (or Treasury) stops creating unbacked paper money, or loans, or checks. (Recession usually follows.)
2. The bank (or Treasury) closes the withdrawal window. No more gold on demand. (Inflation usually follows.)

The second event happens at the beginning of every major war. It did in the United States in December of 1861, when the North invaded the South. It did during World War I when the U.S. entered the war that President Wilson had promised to keep us out of in the election of 1916. They just change the rules. No more gold on demand.

Then they inflate the currency to pay for the war without raising *visible* taxes to cover all expenses.

Since 1933, the United States hasn't been on a gold standard for U.S. citizens, and since 1971, it hasn't been on a gold standard for foreign central banks. This keeps embarrassing runs on banks from occurring as often.

But some day, Mexico or Brazil or some huge-debt foreign nation will default, and the biggest banks in the country will become officially bankrupt. The runs will begin. Then the Fed will step in and create the cash to stem the runs. Fed officials will inflate their way out of the crisis. On that day, you had better own gold, silver, and other similar non-paper assets. The dollar will die.

Summary

As the system of fractional reserve banking has become universal throughout the world, and as the banks have become more vulnerable to bank runs, governments have changed the rules in order to reduce risks for bankers, at least the biggest bankers.

The central banks gained the power to establish reserve requirements: the money that banks must keep on hand against deposits. Then the Fed lowered these reserve requirements. The Federal government abolished the gold standard in 1933. The FDIC was created as an illusion of government-guaranteed bank deposits in 1934. The international gold standard was abolished in 1971, to reduce the pressure placed on the Fed by foreign central banks to give up the gold it holds, supposedly in the name of the Federal government.

And with each reduction in risk for big bankers, they have made wilder and riskier loans. Today, the international commercial banking system has loaned over one trillion dollars to nations and major debtors. The Eurodollar market (a giant, unregulated, almost zero reserve requirement debt market) is over a trillion dollars now. It was under a billion dollars in 1959.

Thus, the world faces a crisis: either more debt to insolvent debtors, or a default. Either more inflation to make the loans, or a giant international bank run. And all of it has come about because the masters of finance and the politicians they buy refuse to honor basic Biblical principles of debt, honest weights and measures, and zero multiple indebtedness.

Economic judgment is coming.

10

A BIBLICAL MONETARY SYSTEM

Owe no one anything . . . (Romans 13:8a).

In Chapter Seven of *Inherit the Earth*, another book in the Biblical Blueprints series, I deal with debt bondage. The Bible regards debt as a form of servitude: "The borrower is servant to the lender" (Proverbs 22:7b).

No monetary system which is based on debt is Biblically legitimate. Such a system enslaves the economy to those who set the monetary rules of the game. If money were not debt money, the Federal Reserve System and other central banks could not exist. The profit-seeking elites that control a nation's monetary policies could not exercise any power at all. The market would determine what is money and what isn't. The market would determine what the prevailing rates of interest should be.

The Biblical principles of money are quite simple:

1 Standard weights and measures, with penalties imposed by the civil government against those who tamper with the scales.

2. A prohibition on all forms of multiple indebtedness by banks, meaning fractional reserve banking.

3. Competitive entry into the silversmith, goldsmith, or any other smith business.

4. No one is to be compelled by law to accept any form of money. (This is not stated in the Bible, but it follows from the first three principles, which are based on voluntarism.) This means no legal tender laws (compulsory acceptance).

The Biblical view is clear: *the State is not to be trusted with the right to issue money.*

103

This is a radical view of money today. It would have been equally radical in any of the ancient empires. They were States that demanded full sovereignty. They centralized power. They claimed to be divine orders. They therefore claimed a monopoly over the issuing of money.

The State that claims the authority to issue money, and especially the sole right to issue money, is claiming the right to misuse the people's trust. Furthermore, throughout history, few States have been able to maintain this right without defrauding their citizens. In fact, there is only one example in human history of long-term stable money: Byzantium (the Eastern Christian Roman Empire: 800 years of gold coins).

Besides, the fractional reserve bankers almost always succeed in gaining from the State the power of money creation. Central bankers eventually replace the State as the dominant influence over money. The politicians are too busy buying votes with tax money to pay much attention to the subtleties of central banking. So State money becomes bankers' money eventually.

Silver or Gold?

One of the common mistakes that amateur, self-taught economists tend to make is to imagine that the value of anything is fixed. "Gold doesn't change in value; everything changes in relation to gold." I have read too many pamphlets that say things like this.

Only one thing has fixed value: the Bible, the Word of God. But even it doesn't have fixed *market* value.

People discover gold. They also find cheaper ways to get more gold out of ore. People discover silver, too. Therefore, the supply of gold changes, and so does the supply of silver. Demand also changes for both metals. So how could they possibly *not* change in value? They change in value every day on the world's commodity markets, and their prices change in relation to each other. Any so-called 16-to-one ratio between silver and gold is a figment of people's imagination; it's a legacy of an early price control of the U.S. government in the late 1700's — a legacy that called Gresham's law into effect, alternately driving out of circulation either silver or gold, depending on which one was artificially undervalued by the Federal government at any point in U.S. history.

The problem is, people think there has to be only one "supreme" money, defined in value by the government. Yet we voluntarily use paper money, checks, credit cards, and token coins: pennies, nickels, dimes, etc. We used to use silver coins, and before that, gold coins. We once used private banknotes, before the Federal government started taxing them, and the banks switched to checks (untaxed).

Why do we think we need one "supreme" form of *State-defined* money? The only State-defined form of money that is legitimate is tax money. The government has the authority to determine what it will accept as payment *from among the various types of privately produced moneys that become established through market competition*. But the State cannot be trusted to establish its own money. It always betrays this trust. It counterfeits its own currency. It inflates.

The U.S. Constitution specifies that gold and silver alone may be issued by the state governments as legal tender currency (Article I, Section 10). The Founding Fathers clearly recognized the limits that metal moneys place on governments. Unfortunately, they neglected to place the U.S. government under a similar restriction. The first great political battle of the Federal government after the Constitution was over the establishment of a privately owned central bank, which Alexander Hamilton wanted and Jefferson opposed. Hamilton won, and the U.S. began its long, though intermittent, history of fractional reserve central banking.

The important point is that the State must not be allowed to establish any fixed price between any two forms of money. I am not speaking here of warehouse receipts that function as a *substitute* for metal money. If a warehouse receipt promises to pay one ounce of gold, it must have one ounce of gold in reserve. I am speaking here of the exchange price between two market-created moneys: gold vs. silver, copper vs. silver, dollars vs. yen, etc. The government must not enforce price controls on anything, including money.

To fix a price between silver and gold brings Gresham's law into operation. The artificially overvalued currency will drive out of circulation the artificially undervalued currency. Gold and silver aren't immune from this law of price-controlled moneys. Governments, including the U.S. government, have tried to discover "the" price between gold and silver, and invariably this has led to the disappearance of one of the two metals. One of them will be artificially undervalued in comparison to what the free market determines. Fixing the exchange value between two forms of money is just another fruitless example of government price controls.

Never forget, there's no such thing as a price control. There are only *people controls*. Price controls in fact restrict what people are allowed to do. It interferes with their freedom.

Similarly, the government is not to set up price controls over interest rates. Interest rate ceilings restrict the voluntary agreements between borrowers and lenders. The State should enforce all moral, legal contracts, and there is nothing in the Bible that indicates that any particular rate of interest is immoral.

The Gold Standard

The gold standard is not *theoretically* preferable to any other *honest* money standard. The only standard that matters is the *no fractional reserves standard*, coupled with the *no false balances standard*.

Gold *historically* has been one of the two most preferred standards, along with silver. It has all the characteristics of money: divisibility, transportability, durability, recognizability, and scarcity (high value in relation to weight and volume). It has been a money standard.

Most important, gold is a rare metal. It is therefore expensive to mine. Not much new gold comes into circulation every year. This keeps its price relatively stable but normally appreciating in relation to mass-produced goods and services. Prices of goods denominated in gold should normally be slowly falling in a productive, growing economy.

Governments should probably collect taxes in gold. Gold is convenient. Income in other moneys can be computed (with market prices day by day, or month by month) in terms of gold. Governments should pay in gold, too.

If the State begins to issue "tax coins," it has begun that slow, grim process of recapturing sovereignty over money. Better for the State simply to specify so many ounces of pure gold, and allow the taxpayer to select the form. If some firm is cheating, the government then has a high incentive to prosecute. It's good for the government to prosecute those who violate the requirement of honest weights and measures.

For the State to say that only gold should circulate is a restriction on individual liberty. For the State to say that only gold is legal tender (a legally mandatory form of money) is also a violation of individual liberty. Let people decide how and what they use as money, provided that no fractional reserves are involved.

A traditional gold standard requires the State to define its official currency in terms of weight and fineness of gold, and then to buy and sell gold at this defined price. This gets the State into the money business. There is no warrant for this practice in the history of Old Testament Israel. The New Testament example is the Roman Empire—not a morally uplifting example.

A traditional gold standard is better than a fiat (unbacked) money standard, but it transfers too much sovereignty to the State. It also allows the State to "change the rules" at its own convenience, that is, to redefine the currency unit (usually by defrauding present holders of the paper currency: less gold per currency unit), or to cease allowing citizens to make withdrawals. Better to have the State policing private issuers of gold and warehouse receipts to gold, and then to collect its taxes in a specified form of private currency. Under such an arrangement, the politicians have a greater incentive to police the State's source of tax revenues than they do to police the State's own monetary practices.

What freedom produces is *parallel standards*. Various forms of money compete with each other. The State is to establish no fixed, bureaucratic price between moneys. The decisions of free men can then determine which form or forms of money become most acceptable. There is nothing magic about money. It is simply *the most marketable commodity.* The market establishes this, not the coercive power of the State. *Money is the product of voluntary human action, not of bureaucratic design.* Money is the product of freedom, and it reinforces freedom.

Banking

What would 100% reserve banking look like? We cannot be sure. Businessmen are creative. They will find ways to cheat, too. But we can sketch the basic outlines.

Most important, there would be no state or Federal charters for banks. The State-granted monopoly of money creation would end. Do-it-yourself banking would become the model. Only one legal rule would restrict banking: no fractional reserves.

What would this mean? First, every depositor will have choices. First, he can deposit his money in a bank for safekeeping, and pay a fee for the service. Presumably, this would be an extension of the safety deposit box function. The bank would segregate these accounts and not allow the money to be loaned out. Not only would no interest be paid on these accounts, but a fee would also be imposed. A "free" service indicates theft somewhere in the system: a violation of the 100% reserve rule. The only way for the bank to profit on such deposits would be through charging the user for services rendered. An obvious service would be check-writing privileges.

Second, there would be another type of deposit from which loans could be made. These loans would be of a specified period at an agreed-upon rate of interest. The depositor might be given a choice: a higher rate of interest, but without the bank's guaranteeing repayment from the lender, or a bank guarantee of repayment, at a lower rate of interest.

The loans would be true loans. There would be no provision for early withdrawal by the depositor. The loaned-out money is gone. Two people cannot write checks on the same deposit, depositor and borrower. If the depositor needed money before the loan came due, he could borrow the money from the bank, using his note as collateral.

Both sides of the loan would be of equal time length. This way, bankers would not be able to "lend long" and "borrow short." They would not be able to loan out money for long periods, yet also guarantee to return deposits on demand. This is what corrupt warehouse owners do when they issue more receipts for gold than they have gold on reserve, and then use gold deposited by one person to pay off the gold withdrawer. Every transaction would be time-specific. There would be no long-term loans without long-term lenders.

This would protect the banking system from bank runs. It would also protect the community from counterfeit money being created by fractional reserve bankers.

Government bank examiners would check the banks in the same way that they check scales of retail sellers. They would see to it that *every loan had a corresponding deposit*. Although the bank would be allowed to pool loans of the same length of maturity (in order to decrease the risk to a depositor that "his" debtor might default on the loan), no *lending* depositor would have check-writing privileges. Check-writing privileges would be offered only to those people who put their money in a fee-for-service safekeeping account.

This may sound confusing, but it's not nearly so confusing as central banking, fractional reserve requirements, the monetization of debt, and other horrors of the modern banking system.

A 100% reserve banking program is simple in principle: something for something, and nothing for nothing. No "free" anything. No impossible promises: "You can write checks at any time against money that we already loaned out, so that we can pay you interest." When you are promised the use of money that has been loaned out, *you know you're getting conned*. When they also pay you interest on the money you can use any time, you *really* know you're getting conned.

If Blondie comes to Dagwood and asks to borrow money from him so that she can buy some new hats, but she also promises him that he can have his money back at any time, plus she'll pay him interest on it, he would probably know better. Even Dagwood isn't that stupid. But he'll deposit his money in an interest-paying

NOW account. Why? Because the bank promises him that there are 5,000 other Dagwoods just as stupid as he is, so they offset each other, and the deal will work.

Just as it worked in 1930-33, when 6,000 banks failed in the U.S. Or just as it worked in the mass inflation of Germany in 1923, when a dollar at the end bought eleven *trillion* German marks on the black market.

Banks and Dominion

The Bible says to owe no man anything (Romans 13:8). This is a good rule for Christians. But it also says that the sign of a God-prospered nation is that people will loan to foreigners, thereby bringing them under some degree of submission.

The Hebrews were allowed to loan money to strangers in the land and foreigners, and still collect payment beyond the seventh year. Why? Because debt is a means to bring other people under your authority. The Bible teaches that evil people should be under the authority of God's law, as administered by God's people. Extending loans to others was a means of dominion.

In times of God's blessings, Israel was to lend abroad. "The Lord will open to you His good treasure, the heavens, to give the rain to your land in its season, and to bless all the work of your hand. You shall lend to many nations, but you shall not borrow" (Deuteronomy 28:12).

In times of God's cursings, Israel would fall into debt to foreigners: "The alien who is among you shall rise higher and higher above you, and you shall come down lower and lower. He shall lend to you, but you shall not lend to him; he shall be the head, and you shall be the tail" (Deuteronomy 28:43-44).

The pattern is clear: extending credit is a tool of oppression in the hands of evil men, but extending credit is a tool of dominion in the hands of God's people. God's kingdom is to be extended over ethical rebels. Ethical rebels are snared and brought under God's authority by means of debt.

But Christians must not be foolish. They must not loan to those unwilling to repay. That would trap them. Their representatives, profit-seeking bankers, will be more careful in selecting credit-worthy bondsmen if the State and State-chartered banking monopolies do not insure bad banks at the expense of the taxpayers.

Christians should be willing to deposit money in 100% reserve banks, thereby allowing non-Christians to learn service through debt bondage. Like apprentices, debt-burdened pagans can learn what it means to work hard for a demanding taskmaster. They will think twice before going into debt again.

Summary

The Biblical case for freedom in money is the same as the Biblical case for freedom in general. The State is to prohibit fraud and violence. The rest is up to individuals.

Fractional reserve banking is fraudulent. It is a violation of the Biblical principle of honest weights and measures. Debasing metal coinage is fraudulent. It is also a violation of the principle of honest weights and measures. Government-issued money is a violation of consumer sovereignty in money. It is a power that the State invariably violates eventually.

Within these general guidelines, "anything goes." Silver money, gold money, platinum money, salt, wampum, anything. Let the buyer decide, and let the buyer beware. Contracts should be written in any way chosen by the parties involved, in whatever form of currency they agree to use.

The development of a Biblical monetary system is based on these concepts:

1. The borrower is servant to the lender.
2. Debt is to be avoided.
3. Money must not be based on debt.
4. Honest weights and measures are to be enforced by State law.
5. Multiple indebtedness is fraudulent, and therefore illegal.
6. Fractional reserve banking involves multiple indebtedness.
7. No one should be compelled to accept any form of currency (no legal tender laws).
8. The State can legitimately establish the form of *privately*

issued currency it will accept as payment of taxes.

9. The big banks eventually capture the control over government monetary policy, so get government out of the money business.

10. There is no fixed value of gold or silver.

11. The State must not fix the price of anything, including the exchange ratios between moneys.

12. Many moneys can exist in an economy.

13. A gold standard has been popular in history.

14. Gold and silver are expensive to mine; hence, they maintain their value relatively well.

15. Traditional gold standards are nevertheless State standards.

16. Freedom of money leads to parallel standards: no fixed price between any two moneys.

17. Bank charters interfere with freedom.

18. For every loan there must be a deposit of corresponding maturity.

19. Banking can become a means of Christian dominion.

20. Christians extend credit; non-Christians borrow.

CONCLUSION

Diverse weights are an abomination to the Lord, And a false balance is not good (Proverbs 20:23).

The question of honest money is really the question of the necessary conditions for human freedom. Honest money is the product of honest people who live and act within the framework of a public law-order that punishes fraud and violence. Honest money requires honest law and people who are self-disciplined. Let the people have what they want, just so long as it is morally valid, non-fraudulent, and non-coercive.

Defining "fraud" and "coercion" is a continuing task of social philosophers. Theologians used to work at it, too, but for the last century or more, they have tended to avoid the difficulties of this task. This is one reason why Christianity has fallen into the historical shadows.

In the past, we have seen brief periods in which relatively honest money has existed. The period of the classic gold standard, from about 1814 until the outbreak of World War I in 1914, is the best example. The wholesale price level in England was about the same in 1914 as in 1815 — a remarkable period of price stability.

While monetary systems were more honest than today during earlier periods, they were not Biblical. There was fractional reserve banking. Also, Gresham's law operated because governments established fixed prices between gold and silver, so "bad money drove out good money." But at least the "bad" money — the artificially overvalued money — was either gold or silver, and it was not easy to mine either one. Geological limits were therefore placed on the rate of monetary expansion. Geological limits were therefore placed on monetary fraud. Governments and banks tampered with monetary weights and measures on a minor scale only.

What does the average person need to remember in order to understand the fundamental principles of Biblical money? Not much.

1. We shouldn't expect something for nothing, such as the depositor's withdrawal on demand of loaned-out funds, or counterfeit money making everyone richer.

2. The State shouldn't interfere with private non-coercive decisions (contracts).

3. It is cheaper to print paper money than it is to mine metals.

4. Money isn't money unless people expect other people to accept it in trade later on, meaning:

5. Money requires *continuity of acceptance* over time.

6. Debasing money is a form of tampering with weights and measures.

7. Debasing money reduces its value in trade.

8. Debasing money therefore reduces the wealth of people who hold money.

9. Warehouse receipts should be backed 100% at all times by whatever is promised by the receipt.

There are other subtle distinctions that are useful, but these are the basics. Any society which enforces civil laws against any violation of fixed, defined weights and measures, and any violation of the rule against multiple indebtedness (unbacked warehouse receipts) will have honest money.

The problem comes when the State, as the enforcer, gets into the business of stamping its mark on "certified money." This process soon becomes money creation, then a monopoly of money creation, then debasing the money, and finally elitist private control over "government" money by central bankers. We have seen this again and again. The control over "government" money by private central bankers is a universal feature of modern economies. So is unstable money.

Monopoly

Men cannot be trusted to possess monopolistic power. No human agency can safely be trusted with absolute power. An absolute monopoly over anything is exclusively God's prerogative, for He alone has an absolute monopoly over everything. All of men's possessions and powers are to be limited.

The so-called "natural monopoly" is very nearly mythical. Very few of them exist. Water in a desert might be one, but most people choose not to live in deserts or walk through them, so such a monopoly is not economically relevant. Almost all economically relevant monopolies are created by, granted by, and sustained by the institution that possesses God's delegated monopoly of violence: the civil government. This is why it is necessary to have numerous competing civil governments. The Tower of Babel was the incarnation of institutional evil (Genesis 11).

The monopoly over money is perhaps the most dangerous of all strictly economic monopolies. Money is the common link in almost all economic transactions. When monopolists tamper with the monetary unit, they send information signals to every participant in the market. When these signals are not created by competitive market forces, they misinform buyers and sellers, savers and borrowers. This misinformation can result in economic crises: mass inflation or disguised inflation (price controls), and then depression.

There is no known way to protect people from erroneous monetary information if money is controlled by the State or by any agency licensed by the State. Only competitive market forces can produce accurate, reliable information on a consistent basis, for competition will put economic pressure on the producers of false and misleading information. People who sell better information appear on the market, and the misinformers start to experience losses.

Thus, what is needed is a market-produced monetary system. Historically, gold and silver have been "the people's choice." This could change in the future. But it is difficult to mass-produce gold and silver. It is impossible to have mass inflation with a currency based on any metal. It costs too much to dig metal out of the ground.

In contrast, paper and ink are cheap. So are blips on computers. If something is cheap to produce, you find that people try to make profits by mass producing it. This is as true of money as it is of hand-held electronic calculators. But additional hand-held electronic calculators constitute an economic asset. Additional money constitutes a redistribution of assets, where the ignorant and vulnerable are most likely to be harmed.

Not Quite Honest Money

It is not my job or your job to tell other people what money they ought to use. It is not the State's job, either.

It *is* the State's job to enforce honest weights and measures, and also to prohibit the issuing of warehouse receipts that are not immediately backed by whatever is promised by the receipt. If the receipt promises to redeem the receipt on demand, there must be an asset on reserve for every such receipt.

If the State does these two tasks, society will have honest money. If it doesn't, society can have only semi-honest money. A traditional gold standard is an example of semi-honest money: fractional reserve banking with full redemption of gold coins on demand. This also involves the government's pledge to buy or sell gold coins at a specified (definitional) price. But bankers cheat, and governments cheat, and the traditional gold standard survived for only about a hundred years, 1815-1914.

The one monetary power that the State legitimately possesses is its right to specify a form of payment for taxation purposes. To that extent, the State can influence the selection of monetary units. But the State does not want to be paid in debased money, so it becomes a watchdog for the public because of its own self-interest in protecting itself from unscrupulous counterfeiters.

For decades, small conservative groups have campaigned for a return to the traditional gold standard. These campaigns have been about as successful as promoting a national treasure hunt for pots of gold at the end of rainbows. They have been futile. They are the equivalent of campaigns to get prayer back into the public schools. They miss the point.

What is the point? Simple: a government-imposed gold standard is not a long-term answer. It didn't work well in the past, and it won't work well in the future. It is still a *government* standard. Our political goal should not be a government-imposed gold standard; it should be the abolition of fractional reserve banking and the enforcement of fixed weights and measures. The goal is to remove the monopoly of money from the civil government and its licensed agents. Nothing else will work to restore honest money. Every other recommendation is a half-way measure. Why devote our lives to half-way measures?

Campaigning for a government-imposed gold standard is impractical anyway. Such a campaign faces tremendous obstacles. First, even the tiny handful of professional economists who favor the gold standard do not agree about which kind of gold standard should be imposed. There are several competing versions. The better versions have fewer promoters.

Second, there is no agreement among the advocates concerning the single most important practical issue: What price should the government set as the official, permanent price of gold? If we adopt a gold price in terms of today's money supply and today's prices, how can we expect the official price of gold to be economically rational when the inflation stops, banks collapse, and prices drop? Will the government have to lower the official price later on —that is, will it have to redefine the currency unit repeatedly? What kind of fixed gold standard is that? But if the money price of gold is kept at the original level, it will be high and rising in purchasing power compared to all other goods. Everyone will then go to the Treasury to sell gold to the government in exchange for paper money, thereby removing gold from circulation and creating a huge hoard of gold in the government's warehouse. Is this wise, placing the nation's gold supply in the care of the State? Isn't this what got us in trouble in the past?

Third, there is no political constituency for any kind of gold standard. The topic is too confusing, and the effects of dishonest government money are not understood by the average voter. The voters are uninterested. It would take a fortune to educate them, and even a fortune would probably not be sufficient.

A New Constituency

Since there is virtually no hope of getting even a half-hearted gold standard back into operation, why waste any further resources in promoting one? Why not assume that there will be a new constituency that will accept and promote a true free market Biblical money system? Why not aim our appeal at this coming constituency? Why not promote the best alternative rather than a compromise that has failed in the past to produce the monetary stability we want?

How will this new constituency come into existence? I would suggest the following scenario. First, the bankers and the politicians will continue to try to make the present system work. This will make the present system worse. Second, there will be a collapse in stages: inflation, then mass inflation, then price controls, then tyranny, and finally a worldwide deflationary depression. At that point, there will be new demand from the voters for answers.

Third—and this is my hope and my prayer—people will at last decide that they have had enough moral and legal compromise. They will at last decide to adopt a simple system of honest money, along with competitive free market principles throughout the economy. They will stop stealing from each other. They will stop trying to get something for nothing politically.

If voters don't experience this sort of repentance, then we will go through the same destructive business cycles again: inflationary boom and deflationary bust. We will be like the fools described by Peter: "But it has happened to them according to the true proverb: 'A dog returns to his own vomit,' and, 'a sow, having washed, to her wallowing in the mire'" (2 Peter 2:22).

There is always one other possibility. Voters will change their minds and demand that politicians change their ways *before* some grim inflationary-deflationary scenario takes place. I think this is unlikely, but the possibility does exist. Voters could look at the arguments of this book and accept them. They could see that something principled is the only way out. They would then bite the deflationary bullet and not let loose until we have honest money. This seems like a remote possibility, but we can hope, and we can pray. Better to go through a principled economic wringer now and thereby avoid the coming unprincipled wringer that is far, far worse in its effects.

We have never had honest money. We have also never had a society fully committed to Biblical law. When we do, we will have at least an opportunity to attain honest money. As the old advertisement said: "Accept no substitutes!"

Part II
RECONSTRUCTION

11

A PROGRAM OF MONETARY REFORM

If My people who are called by My name will humble themselves, and pray and seek My face, and turn from their wicked ways, then I will hear from heaven, and will forgive their sin and heal their land (2 Chronicles 7:14).

What I propose here can be done. It won't be done unless there is a major revival, one which is better informed than any we have seen in the past, but it can be done. I assure you, however, it can't be done at *zero cost*. That's why it won't be done without a spiritual revival.

I'm not a political revolutionary. It isn't my intention to promote a program of reform that will lead to a political revolution.

On the other hand, I'm unquestionably a theological, social, and economic revolutionary. I think that the entire civilization of the West needs to be reconstructed, from bottom to top (though not from top to bottom). I think the rest of the world needs the same thing. But because I'm not a political revolutionary, I believe that this transformation must take place in the hearts and minds of Christians before it can be successfully preached to the world. If Christians refuse to honor their God, why should they expect the God-hating pagan humanist world to honor Him?

Yet it might happen just this way. The pagans might repent before the Christians do. The people of Nineveh repented, and God gave Israel into their hands a generation or two later. The ministry of Jonah to Nineveh was successful; the ministry of the other prophets to Israel wasn't.

It is significant that Jonah preached to the people before he preached to the king. "So the people of Nineveh believed God, proclaimed a fast, and put on sackcloth, from the greatest to the least of them. Then word came to the king of Nineveh; and he arose from his throne and laid aside his robe, covered himself with sackcloth and sat in ashes" (Jonah 3:5-6).

The king wisely asked: "'Who can tell if God will turn and relent, and turn away from His fierce anger, so that we may not perish?' Then God saw their works, that they turned from their evil way; and God relented from the disaster that He had said that He would bring upon them, and He did not do it" (3:9-10).

Where We Want to End Up

The economic point of view takes time to develop. Most humanist economists have yet to develop it, so don't feel discouraged. It takes time.

The fundamental principles of Bible monetary theory are simple enough:

1. Standard weights and measures, with penalties imposed by the civil government against those who tamper with the scales.

2. A prohibition on all forms of multiple indebtedness by banks, meaning fractional reserve banking.

3. Competitive entry into the silversmith, goldsmith, or any other smith business.

4. No one is to be compelled by law to accept any form of money. (This is not stated in the Bible, but it follows from the first three principles that are based on voluntarism.) This means no legal tender laws (compulsory acceptance).

In short, the Bible declares freedom under God's moral law. It declares *freedom without fraud or physical coercion*. Men may do pretty much what they please economically, so long as they avoid fraud and physical violence. There are only a few prohibitions in the Bible against voluntary exchange; these refer to inherently immoral transactions. (My favorite example of a crime which a vast majority of citizens immediately recognize as immoral and illegal is a homosexual who gives heroin to an eight-year-old boy in exchange for sex. If you think the State has nothing to say about this voluntary transaction, or "victimless crime," you are a really *serious* philosophical libertarian!)

Thus, in monetary affairs, we should seek to avoid a monopoly over money, including the State's monopoly over money. We also should oppose the State's transfer of a monopoly over money to a central bank that is owned and operated by representatives of private commercial banks.

The Traditional Gold Standard

Thus, our long-term goal should not be with the return to a traditional gold standard, in which the State issues both gold coins and paper money, promising to buy and sell gold at a fixed price for paper money issued by the State.

It has been a major mistake of conservative economists to think that a traditional gold standard is anything more than a temporary stop-gap. It is easy for the State to destroy the gold standard by issuing either of these announcements:

1. "Henceforth, the new price of gold (new definition of the nation's currency unit) is [such and such more per ounce]." This means an increase in the price of gold—an overnight depreciation of the monetary unit.

2. "Henceforth, the government no longer will redeem its paper notes with gold on demand."

The second edict ends the so-called gold standard. In short, the traditional gold standard is in fact a *paper* standard: the paper of government promises. Historically, these promises have not been worth the paper they're written on.

The First Target: Central Banking

The goal is to eliminate all central banking, meaning an institution operated by and for fractional reserve bankers, but granted a monopoly over money by the State.

Obviously, this is today a utopian dream. But could we begin a program of salami-slicing—a steady cutting away at the Federal Reserve System? I think we can. Step by step, we should pressure the politicians in Washington to take these steps.

First, the Federal government, as a symbolic gesture, should issue to the Federal Reserve System exactly $11,090,000,000 worth of zero-interest-paying, special "good as gold" Treasury bills, and demand that the Federal Reserve System return the *real* gold it bought with its counterfeit money. This will not change the total reserves of the Fed, and therefore will not be inflationary. The United States government will take every ingot of the Fed's reserves out of the vault in the New York Federal Reserve Bank and transfer the gold to Fort Knox, Kentucky, *where it belongs*.

Now, this gold shouldn't stay there long. The government should then begin to sell off every ounce of this confiscated (1933) gold in the form of small gold coins. Anyone who wants to buy them at the market price can do so. All profits on this transaction should go to reduce the Federal debt. But the important thing is to get the nation's gold out of the hands of the Federal Reserve System, if only as an assertion of national sovereignty.

I am assuming here that there really is gold in the official storage centers—Fort Knox and the New York Federal Reserve Bank—and that it hasn't been illegally sold off quietly. This assumption may be totally inaccurate. There has been no official audit of the U.S. gold reserve, since the gold is now supposedly in the possession of the Federal Reserve, and there has never been an official audit of the Federal Reserve System. That is another part of my proposed plan: multiple audits conducted by the Government Accounting Office, the Comptroller of the Currency, and the Treasury Department.

Another possibility for getting the gold back into the hands of the public: simply take the 265 million ounces of gold, melt the gold into one-quarter ounce gold coins, and send four per person to every U.S. citizen. Any coins left over could then be sold.

If the Fed protests, you will know why I say that the Fed now owns the nation's gold, not the Federal government.

Second, Congress should pass a law that requires the Federal Reserve System to submit to an annual audit by the Government Accounting Office and/or any other government-policed auditing agency. Furthermore, all past financial records of the Fed should be audited, with the money for this task being collected from the Fed's interest-rate returns on the Federal debt it now holds.

Third, all meetings of the Board of Governors of the Federal Reserve System must be opened to representatives of the press, to members of the Cabinet, and to members and staff economists of the House and Senate committees that are required by law to supervise the U.S. banking system.

In the case of "emergency meetings" that require "closed-door hearings," the President of the United States, the Secretary of the Treasury, the Speaker of the House, the House minority leader, any member of the U.S. Supreme Court, and the majority and minority leaders of the Senate must be invited to attend.

All decisions of the Board of Governors with respect to monetary policy must be made public immediately after each meeting, not 45 days later.

Fourth, the Federal Reserve System must cease buying or selling any further debt certificates or assets of any kind. A permanent moratorium on such purchases and sales must be imposed. The Fed will not be allowed to inflate or deflate the nation into a crisis, and then demand that we turn everything back over to them.

Fifth, the assets and liabilities of the Federal Reserve System will be transferred to the U.S. Treasury, and the Fed will cease operations entirely. This includes the pension fund of the Board of Governors of the Fed, probably the only fully funded pension system in Washington.

There may be some steps that I have missed. Nevertheless, I would settle for any program of Fed-removal. But the program must lead to Step Five: the abolition of the Fed.

Increased Reserve Requirements

Once the assets of the Fed are back in the hands of the Treasury, control over banking must also reside in the Treasury. The Treasury's task at that point will be to bring the banking system into conformity to the principle of zero fractional reserves, or 100% reserve banking.

To require an immediate return overnight would be to destroy the banks, create a massive immediate deflation, and plunge the world into depression. It would be a violation of contract: banks made loans in terms of a different set of rules. We should not seek revolution.

The government should pass a law requiring the Treasury to enforce a steady increase in reserve requirements for all forms of deposits. It necessarily is an arbitrary number—as arbitrary as allowing people to vote at age 18. We need guidelines, even arbitrary guidelines, in order to make decisions.

Let us assume that an increase of five percentage points per year is selected. In less than two decades, all banking in the United States will be conducted with 100% reserves. Banks and other lending institutions will be required to shift their loan portfolios out of "automatic withdrawal on demand" accounts into "loan my money, and I'll do without it in the meantime" sort of accounts, or else "fee for safekeeping and check-writing" accounts.

This will shrink the money supply, just as the abolition of phony warehouse receipts would shrink the money supply. This is morally and Biblically mandatory. We are today violating God's law. We are using counterfeit money. We need to return to honest money. We need to cease using counterfeit money as the basis of our economy. There is no choice: we must return to honest, "unadulterated" money.

Borrowers had better plan on falling prices. Lenders had better plan for the same thing. Loans will be a lot tougher to pay off. The loan market will eventually impose a price *deflator* tied to the consumer price index. (Loans these days have had implicit "inflators" built into them by the loan market.) The lending rates will discount the expected decrease in prices. Short-term interest rates might get back to where they were in 1933: under 1%.

Deflation will also persuade borrowers to ask for shorter-term loans. This, too, is basic to a Biblical social order: no loans to the faithful for over seven years (Deuteronomy 15:1-2).

Every bank and lending institution, including money-market funds, will come under this rule: no check-writing from accounts that have already loaned out the money. The length of maturity of the deposit will match the length of maturity on the loan. There will no longer be "a substantial penalty for early withdrawal," as the bank advertisements say today, because there *won't be any early withdrawal*. There will be only borrowed money with the original deposit and its interest pledged as collateral.

Buying Off the Bankers

Will the banks scream bloody murder? You can imagine just how loud. One of the most effective political lobbies in the world will go into action. So we offer them a deal. We buy them off.

We tell the bankers, "All right, boys, we all know the mess you're in. You are sitting on top of a mountain of bad debts. You want out. The U.S. government is here to help you weather the storm. We will do a swap. You sell us your pile of Mexican and Brazilian bonds, and we will give you nice, safe 90-day Treasury bills in exchange. You get your portfolios liquid again. We will take all that lousy debt you're sitting on, which you know will never be paid off, and you get in its place interest-paying T-bills. You can even sell them if you want—there's a market for them, unlike those Mexican bonds you're sitting on."

That would bail out the big banks. It would defuse the Third World debt crisis. It would "re-liquify" the banking system. And it would cost the taxpayers only the interest that the Fed now pays on the T-bills it owns. They would go for it.

What about the small rural banks? What's in it for them? Give them the same deal with any remaining T-bills. Swap their lousy farm mortgages for nice, liquid T-bills.

In short, use the reserves of the Fed ($175 billion) to strengthen the banks. Then force the banks to start substituting honest money for counterfeit money.

What would it cost the U.S. taxpayers? Only what they get back from the Fed each year. If the Fed owns $175 billion in T-bills, and they are paying the Fed 7% per annum, then the Fed takes in a little over $12 billion a year. Of this, the Fed will repay 85%, or about $10.4 billion. That's money that the Treasury will have to come up with to pay the banks their interest.

Not bad. For this money—more or less, depending on where interest rates go—the Federal government can bail out the U.S. banking system, wipe out the Federal Reserve System forever, and receive in trade over two decades the re-establishment of honest, 100% reserve banking.

Freedom to Buy and Sell

Deflation will unquestionably cause many more crises, but at least we get started on the road to honest money. If we don't get started, events will force a series of economic calamities on us.

To keep deflation from creating a total depression, every government price restraint must be abolished. Freedom is a package deal. It will do little good to shrink the money supply if people are not completely free to offer their goods and services at any price they choose. The government-created cartels that exist today should lose their privileged status. People must be left free to bargain as best they can, to sell their services at whatever price they can get, and to avoid arrest or fines for trying to get the best deal they can. At the very minimum, this means no more minimum wage legislation.

If the voters aren't ready for this kind of freedom, they aren't ready for honest money. They had better be ready for a catastrophic inflation, followed by a deflationary depression, because that's what the alternative is to honest money and honest competitive pricing.

Summary

I have already said that the Fed's gold should be transferred back to the U.S. Treasury. The Treasury should then sell off every ounce of this gold to the general public in small, affordable gold coins. The money received should go exclusively for debt reduction.

There must be a moratorium on all new Federal debt. There must be a balanced budget, starting now. But there needn't be a gold standard. With respect to a government standard, there needn't be a gold standard ever again.

If we get honest weights and measures, and we also get the banking equivalent, 100% reserves, then we will get honest money. It will be a system that allows gold, silver, platinum, beads, copper, or anything else to serve as money, side by side. The main thing is this: we get the government out of the money business. We end the invisible tax of inflation.

There has been far too much debate in conservative circles about restoring the gold standard. If we have fractional reserve banking, we can't get and keep a traditional gold standard. We never know what is the proper price of gold to re-establish as the official price. None of the pro-gold economists has ever come up with a solution to this problem.

If we don't have fractional reserve banking, and if we do have enforcement of laws prohibiting false weights and measures, we don't need government-supplied money. If we don't have government-supplied money, we don't need a gold standard.

Why not the best? Why not Biblical money? Why confuse the issue by arguing about the re-imposition of a traditional gold standard? Since we don't have the political clout to get a traditional gold standard anyway, why not go for the best possible deal? Why not push for market-produced honest money?

We won't get either, in my view — at least not before we get mass inflation, price controls, rationing, and a collapse of the international monetary system. But we can try. If men refuse to listen, then God, by way of inescapable market forces, will destroy the present fiat money, fractional reserve banking system. One way or another, its days are numbered.

12

THE POLITICS OF MONEY

Therefore the Lord says, The Lord of hosts, the Mighty One of Israel, "Ah, I will rid Myself of My adversaries, And take vengeance on My enemies. I will turn My hand against you, And thoroughly purge away your dross, And take away all your alloy. I will restore your judges as at the first, And your counselors as at the beginning. Afterward you shall be called the city of righteousness, the faithful city" (Isaiah 1:24-26).

The problem with discussing money is that people with only a smattering of knowledge about monetary theory or practice think they know all they really need to know. They hold strong opinions in many cases. Economists are insufferable; everyone else is merely intolerable.

People who would never think of voicing an opinion on organic chemistry have fixed views on money. The number of recommendations concerning the reform of money is legendary: the recommendations go all the way back to the ancient world.

The ancient world didn't come to any clear conclusions, either.

But what about the Christian church? What has it said about money? Not much. It has legislated against "usury" (interest) for a millennium and a half, fortunately with little success. So far as I know, the only people who claim to preach a Christian view of money are a minority of adherents of the inflationist group called the Social Credit movement, an intellectual heir of the old "greenback" movement of late-nineteenth-century America. (The "greenbackers" were proponents of "green"-backed paper money, meaning the green color of the paper, in contrast to gold-backed, fully redeemable paper money, the traditional gold standard.)

I have several shelves of their poorly written and poorly printed tracts, stretching back to the 1920's. They are worthless as economic documents. All they call for is government-issued unbacked fiat money, to stimulate business and stabilize prices. They preach a crude version of the academically popular defenses of fiat money.

The basic debate boils down to this: Is the State a reliable institution to control money, or is the unhampered free market? The "mild" inflationists are always on the side of government-issued money. So are the "stable prices" advocates. Only those who believe that market prices should be *market* prices are advocates of market-produced money.

Thus, those who favor free-market money do not get a hearing, not in academic circles, "monetary crank" (greenback) circles, or political circles. Those who advocate the removal of monetary power from any known special-interest group, especially the State, find few supporters. Everyone wants *his* group to control money—"for the good of the nation," of course.

The American Christian Political Heritage

A century of confusion has misled Christians in the United States. The last self-consciously Christian President was Presbyterian Grover Cleveland, who favored a gold standard, low taxes, free trade, and who vetoed more bills in two terms than any other President in history. (He had been known as the "veto mayor" of Buffalo, New York.) He served two terms, 1885-89 and 1893-97. From that point on, Christian politics slid down the road toward modern statism.

Another theologically conservative Presbyterian, but a political and economic radical, William Jennings Bryan was nominated three times to be the Democratic Party's candidate for President, and he owed it all to his famous "cross of gold" speech of 1896. Almost singlehandedly, Bryan converted the Democratic Party from a gold standard, low-tariff, free-market political party, which it had been since the days of Andrew Jackson (a forceful opponent of central banking), into a pro-State radical party. He ran for the last time in 1908; the next Presidential election saw Woodrow Wilson, also a Presbyterian but anything but a conservative, elected President. Wilson gave us the graduated income tax and the Federal Reserve System.

Bryan was an inflationist. He proclaimed the silver standard as the means for debt-ridden farmers to pay off their debts in less valuable money. (Just for the record, defrauding creditors is never a wise long-term policy.) Later, he helped promote the creation of the Federal Reserve System, and only publicly apologized later when he found that it was owned and operated by the very Wall Street and New York banking interests that he had always hated. He was naive, as well as an inflationist.

Bryan radicalized a substantial segment of Christian voters in the United States. Then his devastating humiliation in 1925 at the hands of evolutionist lawyer Clarence Darrow at the famous Scopes trial (the "monkey trial") in Dayton, Tennessee led to half a century of political hibernation by fundamentalists and conservative evangelicals. (Bryan died a few days after the trial.)

Thus, American Christian thinking on economics is muddled. Christians' "populist" instincts are anti-bank, yet pro-paper money. Christians are patriotic, but with this has come a suspicion of foreigners and foreign imports. They are more like Bryan than Cleveland.

Who Wants the Reform of Money?

Many people want a reform that will favor their special-interest group. The problem is, nobody wants a reform that will remove power over money from all known special-interest groups.

Men want the State to control money, for they believe that their special-interest group can eventually gain a hearing before the money managers, or perhaps even become the money managers. Everyone has the hope that somehow, sometime he and his associates will capture the monopoly of money. Then the world will at last be ruled well.

What nobody takes seriously is that all of us, acting as producers in a competitive free market, are capable of selecting the form of money we want. The special-interest groups don't trust the decisions of the largest economic group of all: *consumers*. Consumers just don't have the wisdom, or the collective power, to force the world to accept what it really needs (if people just understood "how the world *really* works").

Market Knowledge and Bureaucratic Knowledge

The trouble is, nobody knows exactly how the world really works. We are all fallible people with limited knowledge. It is only through Biblical revelation from the One who knows how the world really works because He made it and actively sustains it that anyone can come to a competent understanding of the world.

God has graciously revealed the judicial rules that produce social order, including the institution of the free market. He has established as His standard a law-order which favors the development of competitive markets. Then, through the voluntary exchange of information, and voluntary cooperation among market participants (you and me), we find that we benefit from knowledge that we never even knew existed. Each man brings his best knowledge and skills into the market, and through voluntary cooperation, these skills and information are assembled in ways that meet the needs of consumers.

God therefore has created a system which gives us vast quantities of useful information, yet because it is God-given, man cannot retain this knowledge when he tries to imitate God and control things from the top as a cosmic tyrant. We can possess the fruits of our many insights only when we cooperate with each other voluntarily.

This is as true of monetary affairs as it is of any other highly developed institution. We don't know how everything works as a whole. We don't need to. To try to understand it all is to play at becoming God. What we know is that if we restrain fraud and coercion, the best solutions to our problems of production and exchange will be brought into being. We don't know what these solutions are. All we know is that we don't have them now, and that if we refuse to honor God's guidelines ("blueprints"), we have no hope of discovering them.

The Grab for Power

Men in rebellion against God need to find a substitute source of authority. The State is the place they begin to look, for it has the greatest visible power of any earthly institution.

When they want money, they think to themselves, "Someone is keeping the money I need away from me. Lots of people have money, but I don't have enough. I need to get into control of the money machine."

Now the fact is, as a nation, we don't need more money. We need more per capita productivity. Goods and services make us wealthy, not pieces of paper with politicians' pictures on them. But as individuals, we see that we need more money. What we really mean is: "I need more money, but without my competitors' laying their hands on more money."

The way to get more wealth, the Bible says, is by covenantal faithfulness to God's law, and productive service to other men. In short, the Bible teaches the doctrine of consumer sovereignty. Serve the other person's needs, and you will prosper.

But this is too difficult for people to accept. They want a short cut. The printing press seems to be a short cut. Capture the State, and you capture the printing press.

Karl Marx wrote in his *Communist Manifesto* that one of the ten things a successful Communist revolution must do is to create a central bank. He saw what the private bankers who had set up the Bank of England had accomplished in the way of central power over the economy, and he wanted proletarians to imitate them, or more to the point, the elitist party members who would act in the name of the proletariat.

Marx wanted the reform of money. Lenin wanted it, too. Every special-interest group wants it. Money is power; control over money is a way to get power.

A Political Program for Christians

The average person in the pew is not going to remember all the subtle arguments of a set of books like Biblical Blueprints. Nevertheless, anyone can grasp the fundamental principles of a God-fearing social order:

1. Self-discipline under God's revealed law
2. Avoiding the centralization of power (localism)
3. Service as the principle of dominion
4. Personal responsibility for one's actions
5. The family as the primary agency of welfare
6. Salvation by grace — not knowledge, or power, or law (State legislation)
7. Compound growth over long periods of time (anti-revolution)
8. Neither individualism nor collectivism — *covenantalism* instead

Whenever a Christian begins to think about various specific social, military, political, educational, or economic problems, he has to think through these fundamentals, and then apply them to the specific field of study. This is as true of monetary theory as it is in the other fields.

We have little hope of reconstructing the monetary order strictly or primarily through political reform. Until we can begin to shrink the State as a matter of policy, with the support of the vast majority of the State's present corrupted beneficiaries, we will not see a Bible-based monetary reform.

Will men voluntarily give up the State's perceived benefits? Not without a moral reform which is guided by Biblical knowledge (such as in the Biblical Blueprints books), or not without a near-revolutionary crisis (the judgment of God). God much prefers moral reform and a steady commitment by men to impose His principles in every area of life. That, and *only* that, is the basis of avoiding the judgment of collapse — militarily, economically, and perhaps even medically (AIDS). The disasters described in Deuteronomy 28:15-68 can be avoided only by moral transformation.

But God will not be mocked. The reform will come. It may have to come through economic collapse, which will involve the destruction of the present world monetary system. Then, out of the rubble of broken contracts, broken hopes, and broken State currencies, something better will arise, *if* Christians know what to recommend, and *if* they are in a position to get a hearing.

The best thing about the Biblical principles of money is that the State doesn't have to do much. It can just leave things alone. A team of bank examiners will have to see to it that the banks and other financial institutions are not creating money by issuing the equivalent of unbacked warehouse receipts, but that is just about it. I am not calling for a top-down imposition of a "new monetary order." I am calling only for a bottom-up development of as many monetary alternatives as people are capable of devising and implementing.

Too Easy . . . or Too Hard?

The principled program is always easy to specify. It is not easy to impose. That is the problem: *imposing a program.* A top-down transformation of the social order just isn't possible. People rebel. They learn how to cheat, gum up the works, beat the system. The State spends an increasing amount of its dwindling resources in just gaining minimal compliance, let alone active cooperation.

There is only one way to gain long-term social reform: to convince the average citizen of the *moral correctness* of a *general approach to life*, as well as the *blessings for adherence* to this general approach to life. That is why God included Deuteronomy 28 in His Word: blessings and cursings. That is why He commanded the reading of the whole law every seven years (Deuteronomy 31:9-13): to reinforce men's understanding of the general principles of Biblical law and the case-law applications in daily life.

The law must be *simple enough* for simple people to understand, and *comprehensive enough* for judges to apply to any and every dispute among men. The Bible provides such a law-order.

A successful long-term reform of any institution must gain the understanding and cooperation of those who will be affected by it.

It must be kept simple. It must also work. What we need to understand is that *God's principles work*. They satisfy equally the desires of the moral man and the pragmatic man, the theorist and the activist.

The Biblical principles of money are easy to understand—much easier to understand than the graduate-school textbooks in monetary theory. After all, the textbooks try to explain a morally corrupt system in terms of its supposed long-term benefits, a super-rich elite-controlled system in the name of democracy, and an engine of inflation in terms of historic monetary stability. They try to tell us that there is no reason to repay debt, since "we owe it to ourselves," and besides, the Federal Reserve can monetize it.

Compared to the task of the economists, the Christian's task is easy. All he has to promote is a simple truth: "Don't cheat."

If the Present System Continues

We can look at the inescapable numbers and make some reasonable guesses.

Debt

The world's mountain of debt is growing relentlessly. There is only one answer given by Third World leaders, international lending agencies, economists, and financial columnists: *extend more credit*. Roll over the loans. Make the terms of payment easier. In short, *delay*.

"Delay" is not a viable answer. It is a non-answer. Half of the trillion dollar international debt is owed to Western banks by insolvent Third World socialist nations that have no intention of repaying, and no means of repaying even if their hearts weren't evil. They blame us for their debt, because we loaned them the money to buy our products, which by now they have squandered in waves of socialist pyramid-building. Too bad for us, they say. The stupid gringos lose again. But that's why God made gringos, in their view, the same way He made sheep.

Inflation

The default is coming. The questions then are:

1. How can the politicians disguise the default?
2. How can they blame someone who is politically weak anyway?
3. How can the banks keep their doors open?
4. How can the system be kept going longer?
5. How can citizens be pushed into higher tax brackets?
6. What is more acceptable to voters: outright default with *deflationary* depression, or disguised default with *inflationary* depression?

Most people are in debt. Most people are more concerned about muddling through in the present than in the future. So inflation is the preferred solution. They don't get evicted from their homes; they pay their loans with worthless money. They may not be able to buy another home, nor will their children be able to afford to, but *they keep what they have*.

This is a no-growth, short-future, pagan view of life, but it is the view which debtors want. It is the world which inflation eventually produces.

We will therefore get "default through inflation."

Price Controls and Rationing

To hide the *effects* of monetary inflation — rising prices — governments impose price controls (meaning *people* controls). Shortages will appear in the crucial market areas: price competitive, mass-produced goods. This means that people will be forced to go into the black market to survive (guilt-manipulated, fearful people are easier for the State to control in other areas), or that they will suffer a reduction in their standard of living (making them even more dependent on the State).

The State will probably impose price controls.

Summary

People in debt find it difficult to call for the end of inflation and a steady reduction in the money supply. They fear calling for an end to State-enforced (and mythical) bank account insurance schemes. They fear being visited by the repossessor. In short, if you are in debt, you are hampered in fighting the good fight.

But practically all Christians are in debt. Their businesses are in debt. Thus, I don't expect strong Christian support for my proposed reforms. I expect instead a devastating destruction of the present humanist money system and the world trade system based on it.

The reconstruction is more likely to emerge from the rubble. Buy some gold and silver coins, some basic tools, some durable consumer goods, some dehydrated foods, get out of debt, and pray. If you can, move out of high-risk urban areas. A crisis is looming. When the welfare checks don't buy anything of value, where will you be living, and what will you be producing?

13

THE REFORM OF DEBT

At the end of every seven years you shall grant a release of debts. And this is the form of the release: Every creditor who has lent anything to his neighbor shall release it; he shall not require it of his neighbor or of his brother, because it is called the Lord's release. Of a foreigner you may require it; but your hand shall release what is owed by your brother (Deuteronomy 15:1-3).

The odds against a Bible-based political reform of money are monumental. It would mean scrapping the nation's monetary system. It would mean abandoning 500 years of traditional banking practice. Because of the huge unpayable debt structure, public and private, national and international, a reform of banking along Biblical lines would topple the entire credit structure.

Understand, *this credit structure is going to topple anyway.* The political question is this: *Who will get blamed?* Today's mountain of debt cannot be paid off, and no one intends to pay it off. That's the "genius" of modern economics: *there is not a single school of academically respectable economists that views the entire repayment of all government debt as a moral necessity.* In fact, there is no school of economics that even believes in moral necessity.

Everyone wants *his* debtors to pay *him* off. That is the only commitment to debt repayment that I can find. But when any group is excused from this obligation, then every group is in principle excused.

The Sabbatical Year

The Bible understands men. God set forth laws that would "cut debt off at the pass," in the language of the old cowboy movies. He put a seven-year limit on all debt.

142

The seventh year in Israel was the sabbatical year. There was no planting or harvesting in that year; the land was to receive its rest. "Six years you shall sow your land and gather in its produce, but the seventh year you shall let it rest and lie fallow, that the poor of your people may eat; and what they leave, the beasts of the field may eat. In like manner you shall do with your vineyard and your olive grove" (Exodus 23:10-11).

In that same year, all Hebrew indentured servants were to go free, and they were to be given capital to help them get started again (Deuteronomy 15:12-15). (This apparently did not apply to convicted criminals who had been sold into bondage in order to pay restitution to their victims.)

Finally, and perhaps most important, the whole of Biblical law was to be read publicly to every inhabitant (Deuteronomy 31:10-13). The seventh year was a year of release from debt, work (agriculture), bondage, and sinful ignorance of God's law.

Debt Bondage

"The rich rules over the poor, And the borrower is servant to the lender" (Proverbs 22:7). The man who "mortgages his future" has in principle become a slave. He has publicly announced some version of the following statement:

"I know the future. The future for me will bring more wealth. With this wealth I will pay off my debts. I can therefore increase my lifestyle today by assuming a debt. I know the future so well, that I can say that for X number of years, I will not make a mistake that will bankrupt me."

This is a form of arrogance. The Bible says, "For now we see through a glass, darkly . . ." (1 Corinthians 13:12a). The New King James version reads: "For now we see in a mirror, dimly . . ." In other words, we don't see the future very clearly.

What if a person living in Old Testament Israel couldn't pay? He could be sold into slavery. Only in the seventh year could he get free, unless he could somehow work off his debt. They were commanded by God to take debt very seriously. In principle, the debtor was a servant (slave) to the lender.

The New Testament principle is even more rigorous: "Owe no man anything . . ." (Romans 13:8a). Emergency debt was tolerable in the Old Testament. In the New Testament, God sets forth a standard of personal indebtedness which is designed to keep His people out of bondage.

Why this concern with debt freedom? God wants His people to be mobile. If a new opportunity to serve Him comes along, we are to be "ready to walk." If we are in debt, how can we walk into a lower-paying form of service?

God wants us to be able to exercise dominion. If we are given an opportunity to start a new business, or get a better education, how can we do this if we are tied to a debt? We serve the lender primarily, not God. Sometimes we need to reduce our expenditures today in order to have greater income and responsibility later on. How many middle-management workers are longing to break free and start their own businesses, but are afraid because of their debts?

Third World Debt

The Hebrews were allowed to loan money to strangers in the land and foreigners and still collect payment beyond the seventh year. Why? Because debt is a means to bring other people under your authority. The Bible teaches that evil people should be under the authority of God's law, as administered by God's people. Extending loans to others is a means of dominion.

In times of God's blessings, Israel was to lend abroad. "The Lord will open to you His good treasure, the heavens, to give the rain to your land in its season, and to bless all the work of your hand. You shall lend to many nations, but you shall not borrow" (Deuteronomy 28:12).

In times of God's cursings, Israel would fall into debt to foreigners: "The alien who is among you shall rise higher and higher above you, and you shall come down lower and lower. He shall lend to you, but you shall not lend to him: he shall be the head, and you shall be the tail" (Deuteronomy 28:43-44).

The pattern is clear: debt is a tool of oppression in the hands of evil men, and a tool of dominion in the hands of God's people. God's kingdom is to be extended over ethical rebels. Ethical rebels are snared and brought under God's authority by means of debt.

But what about the modern world?

The Book-Value Game

The insolvent deadbeat governments to which our banks' loan officers have lent your money and mine are now "in the driver's seat." They call the shots. We see today the truth of that old slogan:

> I owe you $10,000. You've got me.
> I owe you $10,000,000. I've got you.

Only they don't owe us $10 million. They owe the West's banks about $500 billion. Not only do they have us, they have us in a death grip. They can bring down the West's economies overnight, or close to it.

The banks have begun to stop lending to them. The banks do allow them to "restructure their debt," meaning the banks extend the day of repayment. Why? Because they expect to be repaid? Nonsense; they know the money will never be repaid. They are playing the big banks' most important game, the *book-value game*.

Would you pay $100 cash for a Mexican bond with a face value of $100? Not if you're smart. You would discount it by 50% or more, since you know it's a high-risk bond. With oil at $15 a barrel, you might discount it by 75%. They can't repay. They have said so publicly.

But if you are a bank, and you are sitting on top of $100 million in Mexican bonds, the government allows you to keep those bonds on the books at whatever you paid for them originally. The regulators allow you to keep them listed at the price you put down in your account books, back when there was a high market value for those bonds (when oil was at $30, and before the Mexican government nationalized the banking system and allowed the peso to fall from 8 cents to one-seventh of a cent). In other words, when you lent them the money before August of 1982. (Less than four years: that's how fast Mexico's economy collapsed.)

If the government required the big New York banks to list their assets at true market value, every one of them would be legally bankrupt: more liabilities than capital assets in reserve. So the government doesn't require them to do it.

But to keep the game going, there has to be an illusion that the bonds are still good. Banks have to get some interest payments occasionally. If ever there were an outright default by the Third World debtors, the game would end — or, better put, it would have to be changed very fast, with full government cooperation. Once the foreign nation says, "We quit. We aren't paying," the bonds fall to zero value. Then the banks do have to write them down to market value. Then there is a true banking crisis.

So the bankers play the game as long as they can. The Third World debtors also play along, just as long as they don't really have to sacrifice, stop inflating, and turn their nations into productive non-socialist societies.

But someday they will get tired of playing the game. They will get tired of being told by the West to "get your economic houses in order, you deadbeats!" And they will say, in so many words, "Adios, gringos!" Then the bankers will have to scurry around and find a new solution.

Some Quick Fixes

I assume that the Fed has some taxpayer-financed aces up its sleeve. The game can go on a bit longer. Let me discuss a couple of them that even I can figure out, and the Fed's economists are employed full-time to think of even better schemes.

The Debt Swap

The Federal Reserve System is sitting on top of about $175 billion in 90-day Treasury debt certificates, the most safe and secure debt instrument in the world (the U.S. government keeps telling us). So, if it looks as though a major default is coming, the Fed could simply swap some of its $175 billion in instantly salable T-bills for the near-dead Third World bonds that the private commercial banks are holding. Of course, the Fed will swap them at the *book-value* of the Third World bonds, not the market value.

Presto! The commercial banks now own the best assets on the market. The Fed owns an equal dollar amount of worthless Third World debt. But this debt is still on the Fed's books at original purchase price book value. No problem!

Is this legal? Sure. The infamous Monetary Control Act of 1980 legalized the Fed's purchase of any form of debt certificate in the world to serve as a "reserve" for the U.S. money supply. The Fed can buy Third World debt, corporate bonds, or anything.

The banks then own the Treasury debt. All interest payments for this debt will go to the banks rather than the Fed. The banks, unlike the Fed, do not return to the Treasury 85% of their T-bill interest payments each year. Thus, the real debt of the U.S. taxpayer will have gone up by a factor of .85 for every dollar's worth of U.S. debt transferred from the Fed to the commercial banks. Yet the account books of the commercial banks, the Fed, and the U.S. Treasury will show zero change.

As I suggested in Chapter Eleven, why not abolish the Fed and let the Federal government do the swap, in order to get the banks to agree to a slow increase in reserve requirements? At least we should get some long-term reform out of the deal.

Using an Intermediary (the "Bag Man" Approach)

The Fed buys debt certificates from the International Monetary Fund and/or the so-called World Bank (the International Bank for Reconstruction and Development), the two biggest "international" foreign aid boondoggles in the West. These outfits then lend the money to the deadbeat Third World governments. They in turn repay this quarter's interest payments (but never any principal) to the West's banks. The two-bit, tin-horn dictators who run these deadbeat socialist nations will of course pocket a few millions for themselves, and therefore agree to play the game a bit longer.

What we've got here is a kind of multinational bank-financed and U.S. taxpayer-financed *retirement program for dictators*. It's a lot better than your retirement program, I assure you. It's tax-free. Unless, of course, the dictator gets shot first. Then your program may turn out to be a better deal.

The End of the Road

These quick fixes only delay the day of financial reckoning. The Third World debt keeps getting larger. It compounds upward. Third World countries seldom repay any principal. They borrow the money needed to pay the interest. Today, we define national bankruptcy as "not being able to borrow enough money to make the interest payments for a full year."

It can't go on forever. Yet the "experts" have offered no solution except to keep making more loans. They have no solution. There is no solution. *The debtors will default.*

So we are back to my original assertion: long-term debt is immoral, and God always brings judgment on those who extend it. We have made bad loans to bad governments for stupid uses. By "we," I mean our political representatives and our financial representatives, the multinational banks.

But, you say, *my* local bank hasn't made loans to Third World nations. Maybe not, but does your local bank buy the CD's (certificates of deposit) of the big multinational banks? A lot of local banks do. If the big banks go down, so do a lot of local banks.

There will be a default. There *must* be a default. God will not be mocked. We have deliberately subsidized evil. We have poured money into foreign *government* boondoggles, and we have bought foreign *government* debt. We have not aided the future-oriented productive businessmen of the Third World. We have financed the socialist bureaucracies that oppress them. We have not put our money into *self-liquidating loans*. We have financed deadbeat governments with their deadweight projects. We will pay the price for our foolishness.

Debt and Mass Inflation

But everyone is in debt. The government even subsidizes it by allowing us to write off mortgage interest payments against our income when we calculate our income taxes. There has been an orgy of debt over the last generation.

Look at the chart, published by the Federal Reserve System. In 1950, total household debt was less than 35% of disposable (after-tax) personal income. Today, it is over 85% of disposable income. This is over a two-to-one increase in one generation. It represents a radical shift in Americans' attitudes toward debt.

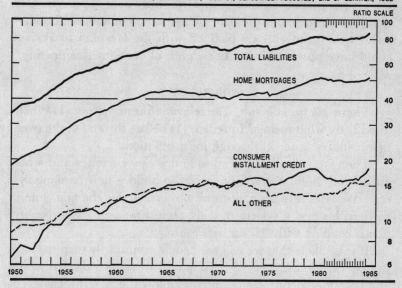

HOUSEHOLD DEBT OUTSTANDING
PERCENT OF DISPOSABLE PERSONAL INCOME
AMOUNT OUTSTANDING; END OF YEAR, 1950-51; SEASONALLY ADJUSTED, END OF QUARTER, 1952-

Because people are so far in debt, they think they can't afford a reduction in money income, even to get a reduction in their monthly expenses. Their debts are fixed in terms of money. A decrease in their money income would lead to personal financial destruction. They fear being evicted from their homes. Thus, politically speaking, *there is no constituency for a return to honest, zero fractional reserve money.* There is no political constituency for deflation. God wants it, but the voters don't. They want "a little" inflation, to help them pay off their debts.

But a little inflation keeps on growing, and anything that

keeps on growing becomes incredibly large eventually, the so-called exponential growth problem. The money supply will balloon. Prices will skyrocket. But this is what people think they need. By destroying the value of money, the government enables long-term debtors to escape. They defraud their creditors with legalized counterfeit money.

At the end of the great German hyperinflation in November of 1923, the mark fell in the black market to eleven trillion to the dollar. One economist calculated that the entire debt of pre-War Germany—mortgages, retirement obligations, commercial bonds—could have been entirely paid off with the German marks you could have purchased with one-eighth of one American penny.

Summary

There *will* be a default. The relevant questions are: (1) When? and (2) By what means? I predict: (1) before the end of the twentieth century; and (2) through mass inflation.

Then we will all be forced to find a new currency and a new currency system. We will be forced to build a new banking system. We will have an opportunity to create, for the first time in modern history, a system of truly honest money: *market-produced monies* coupled with *100% reserve banking*.

It is unlikely that we will see people voluntarily turn to God's principles, for they would be required to reduce their personal and corporate debt to zero, and also allow the government to cut all spending programs and use the money to repay the debt. They would have to avoid all debts beyond seven years. They would have to require the banks to shrink the money supply in response to the imposition of 100% reserve banking.

No one will repay debts with money of today's purchasing power—personal, corporate, or State debts. The personal and political costs would be too high, starting *right now*, and too visible, starting *right now.* People would rather suffer the horrors of mass inflation, shortages, and bankruptcy *later.* They prefer to take the attitude of pagans, the one which Ecclesiastes considered briefly and abandoned in his search for true wisdom: ". . . a man has nothing better under the sun than to eat, drink, and be merry . . ." (Ecclesiastes 8:15b). In short, "eat, drink, and be merry, for tomorrow we die." It is the counsel of bankers and politicians. It is the counsel of despair.

But God will not be mocked. There will come an opportunity for a new beginning, after an international financial crisis of historically unprecedented proportions. The Christian's job is to begin obeying God's laws in advance, to show good faith. A man deeply in debt can be only half-hearted in his commitment to honest, debt-free money. Now is a good time to begin getting out of debt, so that you can in good conscience and full devotion proclaim the Biblical principles of honest money.

BIBLIOGRAPHY

Groseclose, Elgin. *Money and Man: A Survey of Monetary Experience*. 4th edition; Norman, Oklahoma: University of Oklahoma Press, 1976.

Holzer, Henry Mark. *Government's Money Monopoly*. New York: Books In Focus, 1981.

Mises, Ludwig. *The Theory of Money and Credit*. Originally published in 1912. New Haven, Connecticut: Yale University Press, 1953. Reprinted by the Liberty Press, Indianapolis, Indiana.

Phillips, C. A., McManus, T. F., and Nelson, R. W. *Banking and the Business Cycle: A Study of the Great Depression in the United States*. New York: Macmillan, 1936. Reprinted by Arno Press, New York.

Rothbard, Murray. *America's Great Depression*. Princeton, New Jersey: Van Nostrand, 1963. Reprinted by Sheed & Ward, Kansas City, Kansas.

——————. *Man, Economy, and State*. Chapter 11: "Money and Its Purchasing Power." Princeton: Van Nostrand, 1962. Reprinted by New York University Press, New York City.

——————. *The Mystery of Banking*. New York: Richardson & Snyder, 1984.

——————. *What Has Government Done to Our Money?* Originally published in 1964. Distributed by the Foundation for Economic Education, Irvington-on-Hudson, New York.

——————. "The Austrian Theory of Money," in Edwin G. Dolan, editor: *The Foundations of Modern Austrian Economics*. Kansas City, Kansas: Sheed & Ward, 1976.

_____. "The Case for a 100 Per Cent Gold Dollar," in Leland B. Yeager, editor: *In Search of a Monetary Constitution*. Cambridge, Massachusetts: Harvard University Press, 1962.

_____. "Money, the State, and Modern Mercantilism," in Helmut Schoeck and James W. Wiggins, editors: *Central Planning and Neomercantilism*. Princeton, New Jersey: Van Nostrand, 1964.

Rushdoony, R. J. "Money and Society in the Bible," in Hans Sennholz, editor: *Gold Is Money*. Westport, Connecticut: Greenwood Press, 1975.

Sennholz, Hans. *Money and Freedom*. Spring Mills, Pennsylvania: Libertarian Press, 1986.

Skousen, Mark. *The Economics of a Pure Gold Standard*. Auburn University; Auburn, Alabama: Ludwig von Mises Institute, 1986.

Stauffer, Ethelbert. *Christ and the Caesars*. Philadelphia: Westminster Press, 1955.

Taylor, E. L. Hebden. *Economics Money and Banking*. Nutley, New Jersey: Craig Press, 1978.

SCRIPTURE INDEX

OLD TESTAMENT

NEW TESTAMENT

SUBJECT INDEX

WHAT ARE BIBLICAL BLUEPRINTS?
by Gary North

How many times have you heard this one?

"The Bible isn't a textbook of . . ."

You've heard it about as many times as you've heard this one:

"The Bible doesn't provide blueprints for . . ."

The odd fact is that some of the people who assure you of this are Christians. Nevertheless, if you ask them, "Does the Bible have answers for the problems of life?" you'll get an unqualified "yes" for an answer.

Question: If the Bible isn't a textbook, and if it doesn't provide blueprints, then just how, specifically and concretely, does it provide answers for life's problems? Either it answers real-life problems, or it doesn't.

In short: *Does the Bible make a difference*?

Let's put it another way. If a mass revival at last hits this nation, and if millions of people are regenerated by God's grace through faith in the saving work of Jesus Christ at Calvary, will this change be visible in the way the new converts run their lives? Will their politics change, their business dealings change, their families change, their family budgets change, and their church membership change?

In short: Will conversion make a visible difference in our personal lives? If not, why not?

Second, two or three years later, will Congress be voting for a different kind of defense policy, foreign relations policy, environmental policy, immigration policy, monetary policy, and so forth?

Will the Federal budget change? If not, why not?

In short: Will conversion to Christ make a visible difference in our civilization? If not, why not?

The Great Commission

What the Biblical Blueprints Series is attempting to do is to outline what some of that visible difference in our culture ought to be. The authors are attempting to set forth, in clear language, *fundamental Biblical principles* in numerous specific areas of life. The authors are not content to speak in vague generalities. These books not only set forth explicit principles that are found in the Bible and derived from the Bible, they also offer specific practical suggestions about what things need to be changed, and how Christians can begin programs that will produce these many changes.

The authors see the task of American Christians just as the Puritans who came to North America in the 1630's saw their task: *to establish a city on a hill* (Matthew 5:14). The authors want to see a Biblical reconstruction of the United States, so that it can serve as an example to be followed all over the world. They believe that God's principles are tools of evangelism, to bring the nations to Christ. The Bible promises us that these principles will produce such good fruit that the whole world will marvel (Deuteronomy 4:5-8). When nations begin to marvel, they will begin to soften to the message of the gospel. What the authors are calling for is *comprehensive revival*—a revival that will transform everything on earth.

In other words, the authors are calling Christians to obey God and take up the Great Commission: to *disciple* (discipline) all the nations of the earth (Matthew 28:19).

What each author argues is that there are God-required principles of thought and practice in areas that some people today believe to be outside the area of "religion." What Christians should know by now is that *nothing* lies outside religion. God is judging all of our thoughts and acts, judging our institutions, and working through human history to bring this world to a final judgment.

We present the case that God offers *comprehensive salvation* — regeneration, healing, restoration, and the obligation of total social reconstruction — because the world is in *comprehensive sin*.

To judge the world it is obvious that God has to have standards. If there were no absolute standards, there could be no earthly judgment, and no final judgment because men could not be held accountable.

(Warning: these next few paragraphs are very important. They are the base of the entire Blueprints series. It is important that you understand my reasoning. I really believe that if you understand it, you will agree with it.)

To argue that God's standards don't apply to everything is to argue that sin hasn't affected and infected everything. To argue that God's Word doesn't give us a revelation of God's requirements for us is to argue that we are flying blind as Christians. It is to argue that there are *zones of moral neutrality* that God will not judge, either today or at the day of judgment, because these zones somehow are *outside His jurisdiction*. In short, "no law-no jurisdiction."

But if God *does* have jurisdiction over the whole universe, which is what every Christian believes, then there must be universal standards by which God executes judgment. The authors of this series argue for God's *comprehensive judgment*, and we declare His *comprehensive salvation*. We therefore are presenting a few of His *comprehensive blueprints*.

The Concept of Blueprints

An architectural blueprint gives us the structural requirements of a building. A blueprint isn't intended to tell the owner where to put the furniture or what color to paint the rooms. A blueprint does place limits on where the furniture and appliances should be put — laundry here, kitchen there, etc. — but it doesn't take away our personal options based on personal taste. A blueprint just specifies what must be done during construction for the building to do its job and to survive the test of time. It gives direction to the contractor. Nobody wants to be on the twelfth floor of a building that collapses.

Today, we are unquestionably on the twelfth floor, and maybe even the fiftieth. Most of today's "buildings" (institutions) were designed by humanists, for use by humanists, but paid for mostly by Christians (investments, donations, and taxes). These "buildings" aren't safe. Christians (and a lot of non-Christians) now are hearing the creaking and groaning of these tottering buildings. Millions of people have now concluded that it's time to: (1) call in a totally new team of foundation and structural specialists to begin a complete renovation, or (2) hire the original contractors to make at least temporary structural modifications until we can all move to safer quarters, or (3) call for an emergency helicopter team because time has just about run out, and the elevators aren't safe either.

The writers of this series believe that the first option is the wise one: Christians need to rebuild the foundations, using the Bible as their guide. This view is ignored by those who still hope and pray for the third approach: God's helicopter escape. Finally, those who have faith in minor structural repairs don't tell us what or where these hoped-for safe quarters are, or how humanist contractors are going to build them any safer next time.

Why is it that some Christians say that God hasn't drawn up any blueprints? If God doesn't give us blueprints, then who does? If God doesn't set the permanent standards, then who does? If God hasn't any standards to judge men by, then who judges man?

The humanists' answer is inescapable: *man* does — autonomous, design-it-yourself, do-it-yourself man. Christians call this man-glorifying religion the religion of humanism. It is amazing how many Christians until quite recently have believed humanism's first doctrinal point, namely, that God has not established permanent blueprints for man and man's institutions. Christians who hold such a view of God's law serve as *humanism's chaplains*.

Men are God's appointed "contractors." We were never supposed to draw up the blueprints, but we *are* supposed to execute them, in history and then after the resurrection. Men have been given dominion on the earth to subdue it for God's glory. "So God created man in His own image; in the image of God He created him; male and female He created them. Then God blessed them, and God said to them, 'Be fruitful and multiply; fill the earth and subdue it; have dominion over the fish of the sea, over the birds of the air, and over every living thing that moves on the earth'" (Genesis 1:27-28).

Christians about a century ago decided that God never gave them the responsibility to do any building (except for churches). That was just what the humanists had been waiting for. They immediately stepped in, took over the job of contractor ("Someone has to do it!"), and then announced that they would also be in charge of drawing up the blueprints. We can see the results of a similar assertion in Genesis, chapter 11: the tower of Babel. Do you remember God's response to that particular humanistic public works project?

Never Be Embarrassed By the Bible

This sounds simple enough. Why should Christians be embarrassed by the Bible? But they *are* embarrassed . . . millions of them. The humanists have probably done more to slow down the spread of the gospel by convincing Christians to be embarrassed by the Bible than by any other strategy they have adopted.

Test your own thinking. Answer this question: "Is God mostly a God of love or mostly a God of wrath?" Think about it before you answer.

It's a trick question. The Biblical answer is: "God is equally a God of love and a God of wrath." But Christians these days will generally answer almost automatically, "God is mostly a God of love, not wrath."

Now in their hearts, they know this answer can't be true. God sent His Son to the cross to die. His own Son! That's how much God hates sin. That's wrath with a capital "W."

But why did He do it? Because He loves His Son, and those who follow His Son. So, you just can't talk about the wrath of God without talking about the love of God, and vice versa. The cross is the best proof we have: God is both wrathful and loving. Without the fires of hell as the reason for the cross, the agony of Jesus Christ on the cross was a mistake, a case of drastic overkill.

What about heaven and hell? We know from John's vision of the day of judgment, "Death and Hades [hell] were cast into the lake of fire. This is the second death. And anyone not found written in the Book of Life was cast into the lake of fire" (Revelation 20:14-15).

Those whose names are in the Book of Life spend eternity with God in their perfect, sin-free, resurrected bodies. The Bible calls this the New Heaven and the New Earth.

Now, which is more eternal, the lake of fire, or the New Heaven and the New Earth? Obviously, they are both eternal. So, God's wrath is equally ultimate with His love throughout eternity. *Christians all admit this*, but sometimes only under extreme pressure. And that is precisely the problem.

For over a hundred years, theological liberals have blathered on and on about the love of God. But when you ask them, "What about hell?" they start dancing verbally. If you press them, they eventually deny the existence of eternal judgment. We *must* understand: they have no doctrine of the total love of God because they have no doctrine of the total wrath of God. They can't really understand what it is that God is His grace offers us in Christ because they refuse to admit what eternal judgment tells us about the character of God.

The doctrine of eternal fiery judgment is by far the most unacceptable doctrine in the Bible, as far as hell-bound humanists are concerned. They can't believe that Christians can believe in such a horror. But we do. We must. This belief is the foundation of Christian evangelism. It is the motivation for Christian foreign missions. We shouldn't be surprised that the God-haters would like us to drop this doctrine. When Christians believe it, they make too much trouble for God's enemies.

So if we believe in this doctrine, the doctrine above all others that ought to embarrass us before humanists, then why do we start to squirm when God-hating people ask us: "Well, what kind of God would require the death penalty? What kind of God would send a plague (or other physical judgment) on people, the way He sent one on the Israelites, killing 70,000 of them, even though they had done nothing wrong, just because David had conducted a military census in peacetime (2 Samuel 24:10-16)? What kind of God sends AIDS?" The proper answer: "The God of the Bible, *my* God."

Compared to the doctrine of eternal punishment, what is some two-bit judgment like a plague? Compared to eternal screaming agony in the lake of fire, without hope of escape, what is the death penalty? The liberals try to embarrass us about these earthly "down payments" on God's final judgment because they want to rid the world of the idea of final judgment. So they insult the character of God, and also the character of Christians, by sneering at the Bible's account of who God is, what He has done in history, and what He requires from men.

Are you tired of their sneering? I know I am.

Nothing in the Bible should be an embarrassment to any Christian. We may not know for certain precisely how some Biblical truth or historic event should be properly applied in our day, but every historic record, law, announcement, prophecy, judgment, and warning in the Bible is the very Word of God, and is not to be flinched at by anyone who calls himself by Christ's name.

We must never doubt that whatever God did in the Old Testament era, the Second Person of the Trinity also did. God's counsel and judgments are not divided. We must be careful not to regard Jesus Christ as a sort of "unindicted co-conspirator" when we read the Old Testament. "For whoever is ashamed of Me and My words in this adulterous and sinful generation, of him the Son of Man also will be ashamed when He comes in the glory of His Father with the holy angels" (Mark 8:38).

My point here is simple. If we as Christians can accept what is a very hard principle of the Bible, that Christ was a blood sacrifice for our individual sins, then we shouldn't flinch at accepting any of the rest of God's principles. As we joyfully accepted His salvation, so we must joyfully embrace all of His principles that affect any and every area of our lives.

The Whole Bible

When, in a court of law, the witness puts his hand on the Bible and swears to tell the truth, the whole truth, and nothing but the truth, so help him God, he thereby swears on the Word of God — the *whole* Word of God, and *nothing but* the Word of God. The Bible is a unit. It's a "package deal." The New Testament doesn't overturn the Old Testament; it's a *commentary* on the Old Testament. It tells us how to use the Old Testament properly in the period after the death and resurrection of Israel's messiah, God's Son.

Jesus said: "Do not think that I came to destroy the Law or the Prophets. I did not come to destroy but to fulfill. For assuredly, I say to you, till heaven and earth pass away, one jot or one tittle will by no means pass from the law till all is fulfilled. Whoever therefore breaks one of the least of these commandments, and teaches men to do so, shall be called least in the kingdom of heaven; but whoever does and teaches them, he shall be called great in the kingdom of heaven" (Matthew 5:17-19). The Old Testament isn't a discarded first draft of God's Word. It isn't "God's Word emeritus."

Dominion Christianity teaches that there are four covenants under God, meaning four kinds of *vows* under God: personal (individual), and the three institutional covenants: ecclesiastical (the church), civil (governments), and family. All other human institutions (business, educational, charitable, etc.) are to one degree or other under the jurisdiction of these four covenants. No single covenant is absolute; therefore, no single institution is all-powerful. Thus, Christian liberty is *liberty under God and God's law.*

Christianity therefore teaches pluralism, but a very special kind of pluralism: plural institutions under God's comprehensive law. It does not teach a pluralism of law structures, or a pluralism of moralities, for as we will see shortly, this sort of ultimate pluralism (as distinguished from *institutional* pluralism) is always either polytheistic or humanistic. Christian people are required to take dominion over the earth by means of all these God-ordained institutions, not just the church, or just the state, or just the family.

The kingdom of God includes every human institution, and every aspect of life, for all of life is under God and is governed by His unchanging principles. All of life is under God and God's principles because God intends to *judge* all of life *in terms of* His principles.

In this structure of *plural governments*, the institutional churches serve as *advisors* to the other institutions (the Levitical function), but the churches can only pressure individual leaders through the threat of excommunication. As a restraining factor on unwarranted church authority, an unlawful excommunication by one local church or denomination is always subject to review by the others if and when the excommunicated person seeks membership elsewhere. Thus, each of the three covenantal institutions is to be run under God, as interpreted by its lawfully elected or ordained leaders, with the advice of the churches, not the compulsion.

Majority Rule

Just for the record, the authors aren't in favor of imposing some sort of top-down bureaucratic tyranny in the name of Christ. The kingdom of God requires a bottom-up society. The bottom-up Christian society rests ultimately on the doctrine of *self*-government under God. It's the humanist view of society that promotes top-down bureaucratic power.

The authors are in favor evangelism and missions leading to a widespread Christian revival, so that the great mass of earth's inhabitants will place themselves under Christ's protection, and voluntarily use His covenantal principles for self-government. Christian reconstruction begins with personal conversion to Christ and self-government under God's principles, then spreads to others through revival, and only later brings comprehensive changes in civil law, when the vast majority of voters voluntarily agree to live under Biblical blueprints.

Let's get this straight: Christian reconstruction depends on majority rule. Of course, the leaders of the Christian reconstructionist movement expect a majority eventually to accept Christ as savior. If this doesn't happen, then Christians must be content with only partial reconstruction, and only partial blessings from

God. It isn't possible to ramrod God's blessings from the top down, unless you're God. Only humanists think that man is God. All we're trying to do is get the ramrod away from them, and melt it down. The melted ramrod could then be used to make a great grave marker for humanism: "The God That Failed."

The Continuing Heresy of Dualism

Many (of course, not all!) of the objections to the material in this book series will come from people who have a worldview that is very close to an ancient church problem: dualism. A lot of well-meaning Christian people are dualists, although they don't even know what it is.

Dualism teaches that the world is inherently divided: spirit vs. matter, or law vs. mercy, or mind vs. matter, or nature vs. grace. What the Bible teaches is that this world is divided *ethically* and *personally*: Satan vs. God, right vs. wrong. The conflict between God and Satan will end at the final judgment. Whenever Christians substitute some other form of dualism for ethical dualism, they fall into heresy and suffer the consequences. That's what has happened today. We are suffering from revived versions of ancient heresies.

Marcion's Dualism

The Old Testament was written by the same God who wrote the New Testament. There were not two Gods in history, meaning there was no dualism or radical split between the two testamental periods. There is only one God, in time and eternity.

This idea has had opposition throughout church history. An ancient two-Gods heresy was first promoted in the church about a century after Christ's crucifixion, and the church has always regarded it as just that, a heresy. It was proposed by a man named Marcion. Basically, this heresy teaches that there are two completely different law systems in the Bible: Old Testament law and New Testament law (or non-law). But Marcion took the logic of his position all the way. He argued that two law systems means two Gods. The God of wrath wrote the Old Testament, and the God of mercy wrote the New Testament. In short: "two laws-two Gods."

Many Christians still believe something dangerously close to Marcionism: not a two-Gods view, exactly, but a God-who-changed-all-His-rules sort of view. They begin with the accurate teaching that the ceremonial laws of the Old Testament were fulfilled by Christ, and therefore that the *unchanging principles* of Biblical worship are *applied differently* in the New Testament. But then they erroneously conclude that the whole Old Testament system of civil law was dropped by God, and *nothing Biblical was put in its place*. In other words, God created a sort of vacuum for state law.

This idea turns civil law-making over to Satan. In our day, this means that civil law-making is turned over to humanists. *Christians have unwittingly become the philosophical allies of the humanists with respect to civil law.* With respect to their doctrine of the state, therefore, most Christians hold what is in effect a two-Gods view of the Bible.

Gnosticism's Dualism

Another ancient heresy that is still with us is gnosticism. It became a major threat to the early church almost from the beginning. It was also a form of dualism, a theory of a radical split. The gnostics taught that the split is between evil matter and good spirit. Thus, their goal was to escape this material world through other-worldly exercises that punish the body. They believed in *retreat from the world of human conflicts and responsibility.* Some of these ideas got into the church, and people started doing ridiculous things. One "saint" sat on a platform on top of a pole for several decades. This was considered very spiritual. (Who fed him? Who cleaned up after him?)

Thus, many Christians came to view "the world" as something permanently outside the kingdom of God. They believed that this hostile, forever-evil world cannot be redeemed, reformed, and reconstructed. Jesus didn't really die for it, and it can't be healed. At best, it can be subdued by power (maybe). This dualistic view of the world vs. God's kingdom narrowly restricted any earthly manifestation of God's kingdom. Christians who were influenced by gnosticism concluded that God's kingdom refers only to the institutional church. They argued that the institutional church is the *only* manifestation of God's kingdom.

This led to two opposite and equally evil conclusions. *First*, power religionists ("salvation through political power") who accepted this definition of God's kingdom tried to put the institutional church in charge of everything, since it is supposedly "the only manifestation of God's kingdom on earth." To subdue the supposedly unredeemable world, which is forever outside the kingdom, the institutional church has to rule with the sword. A single, monolithic institutional church then gives orders to the state, and the state must without question enforce these orders with the sword. The hierarchy of the institutional church concentrates political and economic power. *What then becomes of liberty?*

Second, escape religionists ("salvation is exclusively internal") who also accepted this narrow definition of the kingdom sought refuge from the evil world of matter and politics by fleeing to hide inside the institutional church, an exclusively "spiritual kingdom," now narrowly defined. They abandoned the world to evil tyrants. *What then becomes of liberty?* What becomes of the idea of God's progressive restoration of all things under Jesus Christ? What, finally, becomes of the idea of Biblical dominion?

When Christians improperly narrow their definition of the kingdom of God, the visible influence of this comprehensive kingdom (both spiritual and institutional at the same time) begins to shrivel up. The first heresy leads to tyranny *by* the church, and the second heresy leads to tyranny *over* the church. Both of these narrow definitions of God's kingdom destroy the liberty of the responsible Christian man, self-governed under God and God's law.

Zoroaster's Dualism

The last ancient pagan idea that still lives on is also a variant of dualism: matter vs. spirit. It teaches that God and Satan, good and evil, are forever locked in combat, and that good never triumphs over evil. The Persian religion of Zoroastrianism has held such a view for over 2,500 years. The incredibly popular "Star Wars" movies were based on this view of the world: the "dark" side of "the force" against its "light" side. In modern versions of this ancient dualism, the "force" is usually seen as itself impersonal: individuals personalize either the dark side or the light side by "plugging into" its power.

There are millions of Christians who have adopted a very pessimistic version of this dualism, though not in an impersonal form. God's kingdom is battling Satan's, and God's is losing. History isn't going to get better. In fact, things are going to get a lot worse externally. Evil will visibly push good into the shadows. The church is like a band of soldiers who are surrounded by a huge army of Indians. "We can't win boys, so hold the fort until Jesus comes to rescue us!"

That doesn't sound like Abraham, Moses, Joshua, Gideon, and David, does it? Christians read to their children one of the children's favorite stories, David and Goliath, yet in their own lives, millions of Christian parents really think that the Goliaths of this world are the unbeatable earthly winners. Christians haven't even picked up a stone.

Until very recently.

An Agenda for Victory

The change has come since 1980. Many Christians' thinking has shifted. Dualism, gnosticism, and "God changed His program midstream" ideas have begun to be challenged. The politicians have already begun to reckon with the consequences. Politicians are the people we pay to raise their wet index fingers in the wind to sense a shift, and they have sensed it. It scares them, too. It should.

A new vision has captured the imaginations of a growing army of registered voters. This new vision is simple: it's the old vision of Genesis 1:27-28 and Matthew 28:19-20. It's called *dominion*.

Four distinct ideas must be present in any ideology that expects to overturn the existing view of the world and the existing social order:

> A doctrine of ultimate truth (permanence)
> A doctrine of providence (confidence)
> Optimism toward the future (motivation)
> Binding comprehensive law (reconstruction)

The Marxists have had such a vision, or at least those Marxists who don't live inside the bureaucratic giants called the Soviet Union and Red China. The radical (please, not "fundamentalist") Muslims of Iran also have such a view.

Now, for the first time in over 300 years, Bible-believing Christians have rediscovered these four points in the theology of Christianity. For the first time in over 300 years, a growing number of Christians are starting to view themselves as an army on the move. This army will grow. This series is designed to help it grow. And grow tougher.

The authors of this series are determined to set the agenda in world affairs for the next few centuries. We know where the permanent answers are found: in the Bible, and *only* in the Bible. We believe that we have begun to discover at least preliminary answers to the key questions. There may be better answers, clearer answers, and more orthodox answers, but they must be found in the Bible, not at Harvard University or on the CBS Evening News.

We are self-consciously firing the opening shot. We are calling the whole Christian community to join with us in a very serious debate, just as Luther called them to debate him when he nailed the 95 theses to the church door, over four and a half centuries ago.

It is through such an exchange of ideas by those who take the Bible seriously that a nation and a civilization can be saved. There are now 5 billion people in the world. If we are to win our world (and these billions of souls) for Christ we must lift up the message of Christ by becoming the city on the hill. When the world sees the blessings by God upon a nation run by His principles, the mass conversion of whole nations to the Kingdom of our Lord will be the most incredible in of all history.

If we're correct about the God-required nature of our agenda, it will attract a dedicated following. It will produce a social transformation that could dwarf the Reformation. This time, we're not limiting our call for reformation to the institutional church.

This time, we mean business.

Jesus said to "Occupy till I come." But if Christians don't control the territory, they can't occupy it. They get tossed out into cultural "outer darkness," which is just exactly what the secular humanists have done to Christians in the 20th century: in education, in the arts, in entertainment, in politics, and certainly in the mainline churches and seminaries. Today, the humanists are "occupying." But they won't be for long. *Backward, Christian Soldiers?* shows you why. This is must reading for all Christians as a supplement to the *Biblical Blueprints Series*. You can obtain a copy by sending $1.00 (a $5.95 value) to:

> Institute for Christian Economics
> P.O. Box 8000
> Tyler, TX 75703

_____
name

_____
address

_____
city, state, zip

_____
area code and phone number

Dr. Gary North
Institute for Christian Economics
P.O. Box 8000
Tyler, TX 75711

Dear Dr. North:

I read about your organization in your book, *Honest Money.* I understand that you publish several newsletters that are sent out for six months free of charge. I would be interested in receiving them:

☐ *Biblical Economics Today*
Christian Reconstruction
and Dominion Strategies

Please send any other information you have concerning your program.

_____
name

_____
address

_____
city, state, zip

_____
area code and phone number

☐ Enclosed is a tax-deductible donation to help meet expenses.

The *Biblical Blueprints Series* is a multi-volume book series that gives Biblical solutions for the problems facing our culture today. Each book deals with a specific topic in a simple, easy to read style such as economics, government, law, crime and punishment, welfare and poverty, taxes, money and banking, politics, the environment, retirement, and much more.

Each book can be read in one evening and will give you the basic Biblical principles on each topic. Each book concludes with three chapters on how to apply the principles in your life, the church and the nation. Every chapter is summarized so that the entire book can be absorbed in just a few minutes.

As you read these books, you will discover hundreds of new ways to serve God. Each book will show you ways that you can start to implement God's plan in your own life. As hundreds of thousands join you, and millions more begin to follow the example set, a civilization can be changed.

Why will people change their lives? Because they will see God's blessings on those who live by His Word (Deuteronomy 4:6-8).

Each title in the *Biblical Blueprints Series* is available in a deluxe paperback edition for $6.95, or a classic leatherbound edition for $14.95.

The following titles are scheduled for publication in 1986:

- Introduction to Dominion: Biblical Blueprints on Dominion
- Honest Money: Biblical Blueprints on Money and Banking
- Who Owns the Family?: Biblical Blueprints on the Family and the State
- In the Shadow of Plenty: Biblical Blueprints on Welfare and Poverty
- Liberator of the Nations: Biblical Blueprints on Political Action
- Inherit the Earth: Biblical Blueprints on Economics
- Chariots of God: Biblical Blueprints on Defense
- The Children Trap: Biblical Blueprints on Education
- Entangling Alliances: Biblical Blueprints on Foreign Policy
- Ruler of the Nations: Biblical Blueprints on Government
- Protection of the Innocent: Biblical Blueprints on Crime and Punishment

Additional Volumes of the Biblical Blueprints Series are scheduled for 1987 and 1988.

Please send more information concerning this program.

---

name

---

address

---

city, state, zip

Dominion Press • P.O. Box 8204 • Ft. Worth, TX 76124